TRANCE

A maker of idols is never an idolater.

OLD CHINESE SAYING

Dennis R. Wier

Trance

from magic to technology

TRANS MEDIA
ANN ARBOR, MICHIGAN

Copyright © 1996 Dennis R. Wier

Publisher's Cataloging-in-Publication Data
(Prepared by Quality Books Inc.)

Wier, Dennis R.
    Trance : from magic to technology / Dennis R. Wier
    p. x cm.
    Includes bibliographical references and index.
    ISBN 1-888428-37-6 (hardback)
    ISBN 1-888428-38-4 (paperback)

    1. Trance. 2. Hypnosis. 3. Meditation. 4. Magic. I. Title.

BF1321.W54 1996   133.9
                                                   QBI95-20830

Library of Congress Card Catalog Number 95-62295

Printed in the United States of America

The paper used in this publication meets the minimum requirements of the American National Standard for Permanence of Paper for Printed Library Materials. ANSI Z39.48-1984.

1 3 5 7 9 10 8 6 4 2

Trans Media, Inc.   SAN 298-8569
317 South Division, Suite 50
Ann Arbor MI 48104

For information about the activities of The Trance Institute, contact:

The Trance Institute, Inc.
Sunnehaldenstrasse 7
CH-8311 Brütten, Switzerland
FAX +41-52-347 1012
Internet: info@trance.ch
http://www.trance.ch/trance/index.html

Contents

Preface

When I was ten years old, I was fascinated by mathematics and anxious to escape listening to my parents argue. I learned that by focusing my mind on solving algebra problems I could enter into a beautiful universe where tough problems had possible solutions. My interest was so intense and my concentration so deep that even though my father might come into my room, talk or ask me questions, I would have no recollection at all of his even entering my room. Both my father and I were surprised that this occurred, and, when it occurred regularly, it was accepted as normal, part of my personality, and forgotten.

Later, in college, I found that I could do my best work in noisy cafes. I did not realize at that time that my power of concentration was a form of trance.

When I began the practice of meditation (transcendental meditation) in 1965 I found that I liked to meditate, and I often jokingly called myself a "meditation junkie." After several years of meditation practice, I began to teach meditation. I became fascinated by these "altered states of consciousness" as they began to be called. I went to India three times to learn more about yoga, mantras and deep meditation techniques from various yogis, swamis, lamas and sufis.

At some point, I discovered "magic." I found that by setting up some patterns, doing some meditation and then breaking the patterns that it was possible to "cause" things to happen in reality. I was intrigued but frightened of this discovery, and I decided not to use it in my personal life. I did, however, write a short paper called *Homotopy and Cybernetics* which made the connection between trance states, magic and certain physical patterns.

While pursuing my profession as a computer software developer, I realized that I had become addicted to computers, and, in a certain way, to all hightech toys. Some of my colleagues were profoundly addicted and would spend long continuous hours in a deep trance creating software, debugging programs, and inventing neat software tools. I watched their physical, mental and emotional conditions deteriorate as they preferred a relationship to a computer to a relationship with a person. My brilliant colleagues in their technical trances looked and smelled like bathless streetpeople or hopeless drug addicts. Partly because of my interest in addiction, I started a newsletter called *Technophiliacs Anonymous*, which addressed the problem of addiction to technology. After a few issues, I began to realize that addiction and trance were very much related. In 1990, my investigation into trance began in earnest.

During the decades of the 80's and 90's, in many parts of America, the interest in magic and shamanism increased. I feel that the model for trance I describe here is both precise enough and rich enough to be used as a type of trance engineering technology with practical applications in many social and psychological areas as well as in religion, spirituality, magic and the occult.

Meditation is a tool of the New Age pagans. Drug and alcohol problems are everywhere in part because the nature of addiction has not been well understood. The world is becoming more nationalistic, and there are constant reports of cults and fanatics gone berserk.

I know that what seems to be unrelated phenomena — magic, addiction, nationalism, meditation states — are actually only some of the natural effects of trance. What I am trying to do with this book is to show what I feel are the relationships between these phenomena and their common basis according to my definition of trance.

This book is basically the product of my own interests and inclinations. It was written to express what I feel must be true about trance. I waited for a long time before writing this as I was certain that what I knew must be common knowledge somewhere. Perhaps it is, but I was not able to discover a clear expression anywhere of the general relationships I feel are obvious to me, nor could I find a forum for presenting my ideas about trance and my model for trance. So, I thought that perhaps I should write down my observations and ideas in a fuller way and people who are interested in trance could make of it what they will. I must state that my model has grown out of my own personal inner perceptions and realizations and not from any particularly specific scientific or academic research. This is one of the reasons the model is highly speculative. So be it.

Dennis R. Wier
Brütten, Switzerland
24 November 1994

The Magic and Mystery of Trance

Since 1965 I have been engaged in the research of trance - privately, personally and practically - although during this time I was not always aware that it was trance I was researching. And I use the word *research* not in a particular scientific or academic sense, but more in an empirical sense.

The results of my research in trance come directly from my personal meditation experience over the past 30 years. Describing one's personal experience of meditation is not easy. Explaining what that experience is about is even more difficult because spoken or written language is not an efficient vehicle for describing subtle, delicate and ephemeral inner phenomena. Explaining why a specific inner experience occurred is even more tricky, first because it is subjective and second because the reasoning of causes lacks objectivity. What I have done here is to use my skills in systems analysis to analyze my inner experiences and to express the results of this analysis in some type of rigorous way. My professional background as a computer systems analyst may tend to make this book seem a bit technical in places. Indeed, what I have attempted to do in this book is to analyze — in a systems analytical way — my own personal realizations — through 30 years of meditation — as to what a 'trance' is.

I assume that an arcane subject as trance might have a limited readership. Many mystic types are likely not to be systems analysts, although some are. Many psychologists these days are *social* psychologists although some are not. Often psychologists have little deep meditation experience, and although many use word processors, they are likely not to be familiar with practical systems analytical techniques. In addition, because trance is a potentially controversial subject insofar as I am discussing magic, shamanism and witchcraft and so on, in the same pages as I describe a technical model for trance, some academic psychologists may perfunctorily dismiss this entire work as unscientific or superstitious. I hope they keep an open mind.

The magicians, shamans, channellers and witches — those who have practical experience with trance — might not appreciate what they may perceive as my lack of a proper or traditional appreciation for or mention of earth Spirits, Gods and Goddesses and so on. It is true that I do not make many references to God or to various spirits, but one important result of my theory is that the practical experience of trance can now be disconnected from all those traditional associations. I humbly suggest that those with deep practical experience with traditional trance practices examine their belief systems in light of trance theory and ask themselves if they are examples of good trance engineering practices.

I can also understand that it might not be very interesting for a witch to read technical material but I feel that understanding some of the technical aspects of trance can immeasurably help a witch to accomplish her goals.

There are many people, institutions and organizations in this world who have a long-term vested and even a vital interest in maintaining and protecting certain beliefs or trances. To disturb these beliefs or trances is certainly not my intent, but it is inevitable that understanding how trance works will have two effects. First, for those who create trances, understanding trance theory will enable them to make better, stronger, more compelling and more interesting trances. Second, for those who are entranced, understanding trance theory will show them what they must do to break trances and how to avoid becoming ensnared by them. No one can escape a trance who has either desire or fear, and this is true for both those who create trances as well as for those who are entranced.

This book is a bit abstract and there are only a few practical exercises mentioned. Indeed, I have not set about here to make any new age trance psychology self-help workbook. What my intent was — and still is — is to express as clear as I can some of the basic ideas of my model for trance. For me, a technical and analytical description is the best way, but I realize that this description might not be for everyone. I can only say that you don't need to be a mathematician in order to understand the concepts, but if you want a precise exposition of my trance theory, I have done my best to provide one here. I have tried to present my ideas about trance simply and simultaneously on several balanced levels while maintaining a consistent clarity of presentation in line with my personal experience.

Trance is an interesting subject for several reasons. First, trance is a phenomenon which can be discovered everywhere, and in nearly any social situation, if you know what to look for. Second, until now, there was no model for trance, so trances were difficult to identify or to classify; the difficulty in identifying trance has given rise to a certain mystery about what a trance was. Furthermore, many people have abused trance and therefore it has a certain negative reputation — no doubt originally from Mesmer, Svengali and Rasputin. Indeed, for some people, just to mention the word *trance* gets them nervous. Often, the reason for this reaction is the association of the loss of volition with trance. What can be more unnerving than something you can't explain, like an unknown mysterious power, which has the potential for making you weak-willed?

Trance is also interesting because traditionally it is an important component of ancient, primitive and modern religious, ritualistic and magical practices. Certainly many ancient priests, as well as modern day western mystics, channels, yogis, techno-shamans and witches would be less in touch with the sources of their knowledge without practicing some sort of trance through meditation, ritual, dance or music. In spite of the fact that all meditation practices use trance-inducing procedures, it is clear to me that most meditators have only vague ideas about what they are doing with trance and have no knowledge of the theoretical basics of trance let alone the extent of potential effects. Many meditators might insist that meditation is not a trance because of the bad connotations of the word *trance* and because they lack the technical knowledge this book provides in order to recognize what they are doing when they meditate. Some religious meditation teachers believe that if you meditate long enough you will get lucky and 'have grace', but they themselves do not know *why* you get lucky.

Once you know what a trance is and how it is produced, it will be obvious that all meditation practices invoke trance. By all, I mean from the yogis in the Himalayas to the new-age gurus and western yogis, witches, shamans, techno-wizards and even those who use trance but do not call it *trance*. Most meditators have no theoretical model for their practice; generally they do not need to understand how or why meditation works. They just need to do it and it works. It is certainly possible to meditate for decades without knowing how meditation works, just as it is possible to drive a car without knowing how it works.

Just as you can be a better and safer driver if you learn some of the underlying technology of automotive engineering, you can also be a better and safer meditator by learning some of the underlying technology of trance. Likewise, if you are a shaman or channeller who enters into trance to contact plant or other energies, it makes a lot of sense to understand what you are doing so that you can do it better and safer.

If you are a practicing monk, priest, yogi, witch or a magician you know that many of your practices involve willful ritual and both inner and outward repeated actions. Reevaluating these processes with trance theory will improve your technique and help make these processes more effective.

Once you are aware of the essential conditions for trance then the effects of trance do not need to be put in terms that have nothing to do with the underlying technology. Like a sophisticated car driver you will become aware that the color scheme of the car or the softness or smells of the interior leathers have nothing to do with its basic automotive functions.

Just as automotive engineers have a certain responsibility towards those who use their creations, those who knowingly create trances for others also bear a certain responsibility towards those who come under their influence. I hope to make you aware that among the many worldwide organizations and institutions which promote or maintain certain beliefs and trances, there are many who practice what we might call unsafe trance engineering techniques. One question that should be seriously asked is: To what extent should people and organizations be liable for the results of their consciously created trances?

Trance is used in many forms of contemporary psychotherapy. The model of trance I describe here will have practical implications for therapists and others who use trance in medical or psychotherapeutic settings.

What makes trance even more interesting is that it is so controversial. There still are some psychologists who claim that *there is no such thing as hypnosis.* In part, and perhaps for good reason, there has not been any consistent and well-accepted definition for *trance.* What I hope to do in this book is to define and describe trance in such a way and with such precision that it will be relatively easy to determine when a trance is, or is not. Perhaps then research can proceed in a more robust way to explore the differences in the types of trances that exist, rather than debate whether there is such a thing as a trance or not. That is, if the model is good at all, it can be used as a practical analytical tool; and, the model can be refined as needed in the future.

I would like to point out that the model is not a social psychological one, but perhaps more like a cognitive behavioral one, and it might provide a theoretical basis for future research into trance phenomena.

I would like to give you some of my personal research history with regard to trance.

I did not begin my research into trance with a hypothesis about trance. I was more interested in learning what characterized advanced meditative states. Over a period of several decades of meditation, I experienced deep meditative states. I realized that these deep states have specific and unusual characteristics, but I did not know how to describe them specifically nor what they were. Were these states a so-called *altered state of consciousness*? Was it hypnosis? Was it merely an hallucination? I really loved to meditate. Was this state then the result of some type of psychic addiction? As the years went by, I also realized that I had to admit that I was personally addicted to meditation. Because of this realization, I concluded that addiction must share some commonality with meditative states. This observation was intriguing to me, because I felt that a state of deep meditation was a desirable condition and, on the contrary, an addiction was a condition to be avoided.

I began to look for the common characteristics of meditative states, trance and addictions. I quickly realized that there was neither a well-accepted model for meditation states nor for addiction nor for trance. Because it seemed intuitive to me that they might be related, I came to the conclusion that both meditation and addiction might be types of trances, but I didn't really know what a trance was either.

I thought that surely if anyone knew what a trance was, it should be the psychologists who have studied hypnosis. I thought that psychologists accept the phenomena of hypnosis and use trance as a therapeutic and investigative tool. I quickly discovered, however, that they could not define *trance* in a rigorous way either. I was looking for a specification of trance every bit as rigorous as I would expect from a specification of a computer application.

What I found was that the subject of hypnosis and trance is full of controversy; some psychologists claim that hypnotic trance can be explained by other social phenomena, and therefore argue that there is no such thing as hypnosis. In spite of this controversy, I began to study whatever hypnosis might or might not be, and from there my investigations led me to study NLP informally and then to study hypnotic theory and phenomena in general and in passing to learn a bit of the history of hypnotism and to read some current research.

I was not insensitive to the fact that deep trances can have profound effects on reality; this has been proven to me multiple times personally through my own practice of meditation. Moreover, one of the reasons a theory for hypnosis or trance is so difficult to design is that such theories must explain certain physiological phenomena that seem to border on magic, such as making warts appear and disappear, or enabling subjects to remember past lives, or display knowledge of events they could not have possibly perceived by the ordinary senses, or exhibiting physical strength or mental skills not normally within their abilities. Those who have perfected the ability to go into deep trance and utilize these abilities seemingly at will have held a fascination by the scientific community, the religious as well as for ordinary folks for thousands of years.

I knew that if I pursued my investigation, I was getting into areas that are full of mystery, controversial and highly charged: meditation, hypnosis, addiction, trance, altered states of consciousness, magic, witchcraft, religion and social control psychology. With my systems analytical professional perspective tuned to require rigorous specifications sufficient to design a computer system, what I discovered written by psychologists about trance and hypnosis didn't make a whole lot of sense.

What is a *trance*? According to the dictionary, a trance is a "daze or a stupor, a prolonged and profound sleep-like condition or a state of mystical absorption." Some psychologists define trance as a state of aroused attentive focal concentration with diminished peripheral awareness. In general, a trance is defined as a state of limited awareness. These old definitions might be workable for some people, but it is wholly inadequate as a really precise or practical definition.

In most ways these definitions are simply misleading. Yet, these definitions are a good place to start as any in order to build up a more precise definition, in spite of the fact that these definitions do not address the issue of the connection between trance and the underpinnings of reality of interest to yogis, shamans and witches among others.

If a trance is a state of limited awareness, then the types of trance would include, but would not be limited to, concentration, meditation, addiction, hypnosis and perhaps include psychotic delusional states. Implied literally by the definition is that anything short of enlightened awareness is trance.

In every type of ordinary consciousness there is always some form of *limited awareness*. When you are concentrated on a problem your awareness is necessarily limited to the problem. When you read a book, this one, for example, you must be in a type of light trance. In meditation states, the attention is generally inward and the limit then excludes the world, often including the awareness of your own body. In addictions the awareness is circumscribed by behavioral impoverishment. In hypnosis, the attention is on the hypnotist. Psychotics have limited awareness as well; therefore it could be argued that psychotics are in a trance of some sort. Sleep itself is a limitation of awareness; therefore, from this old definition, sleep is also a trance. You can probably think of many other social and psychological behaviors that would satisfy the definition of trance as a state of limited awareness. In every case of these types of trance, the definition seems to work: there *is* a so-called *limitation of awareness*. If we include every case of limited awareness as being evidence of a trance, then we must surely either revise our intuitive ideas about trance or make the definition more precise.

What is wrong with this definition is that a limitation of awareness is both an essential component of trance, as well as an effect of trance. Therefore, to define trance in terms of any limitation of awareness is not really helpful from a systems point of view because it mixes the cause of the condition with its effect.

What is helpful in order to understand trance is to conceptually separate that which is done in order to create a trance from the known results or effects of that trance. So, we shall first look at what ways a trance is created, how we do it, and second, we shall catalog and characterize what happens in a trance and what the effects are and see if we can classify the effects in some way.

To make this analysis we will need to make many assumptions and leaps. But these assumptions will hopefully all be made explicit, and I will try to require you to make few leaps of faith. I must caution you, however, that the model for trance which I propose here should be described as highly speculative from a scientific or academic point of view since I make many assumptions about cognitive processes which may be only partially known at this time. There is currently among the cognitive behavioral types a big discussion as to what *consciousness* is. I avoid this controversy by calling it awareness which I never define. I am aware of these controversies, but I am not attempting to resolve that particular controversy.

It may be that the model does not necessarily add new knowledge. What the model does is to offer an explanation of certain types of well-known and simple phenomena. It is fairly well known that if you repeat some thought often enough then it eventually becomes boring and you think about something else. We don't need to know what *consciousness* is to be aware of this rather mundane and common experience.

The model proposes that the mechanism of repeating a limited set of thoughts is the fundamental mechanism for creating a rather large but specific class of trance. The model basically describes this mechanism and then explores some of the implications.

In order to discuss the idea of a limitation of awareness more precisely, let us borrow some mathematical ideas and assume that any limit can be described by a boundary of some sort which circumscribes a space. This boundary is in a state of flux but is always closed dividing the space in two. Moreover, there is an implication that the boundary constitutes a type of measure on the topology of the closed space. That is, somehow we can describe how big it is and how it changes, as though it were a type of surface.

In a trance, the thoughts which exist within a boundary of awareness tend to repeat. That is to say, when a boundary severely limits choice for a sustained period of time, then the clinical characteristic of trance will become more prevalent. Large boundaries also contain patterns of repeated thoughts. But, because a repetition is not frequent in such large boundaries of awareness trances are not usually identifiable as such.

Although my specific interest is in the boundaries which exist in *human* cognition, it is important to touch the toes of the largest boundary which circumscribes the trance we all live in. Ancient Vedic philosophers identified the largest boundary of all as the *mahamaya*: the Great Illusion or Universal Trance. The Mahamaya is the Reality that we all live in, and it is also a trance, although it is a very big one we all we all seem to share.

The Importance of Trance

Although the Mahamaya or Universal Trance is important in philosophical as well as in a magical sense, most of us do not operate on those abstract, mystical, magical or philosophical levels. Let us set it aside for a moment while we continue to develop the fundamental characteristics of trance because what we discover on the personal level, inside us, probably has implications on the universal level as well.

Within this Mahamaya there are a great number of choices. The choices are everything that may exist. It may be difficult to recognize the entire Reality as a trance, so let's go to the other end of the spectrum where choice is limited to two.

When a car salesman is trying to sell you something he does not tell you to chose between buying and not buying. He tells you to chose between the green car and the blue car. By limiting your choices the salesman enables your action and potentially frees your money energy.

A salesman may convince you by the skillful use of many trance-inducing strategies. He may discourage your natural inclination to explore a wider range of possibilities or belittle other possibilities and he may associate pleasant personal memories with the choices he wants to give you. He may claim, for example, that driving the green car is like remembering when you were playing in a shimmering field of green grass on that lovely warm summer day. At the conclusion of his induction you may really feel that the only reasonable choice should be between the green one and the blue one and you really do prefer the green car. At that moment you are in a trance, you have lost your will power and your judgment has been violated along with your memory.

You make an arbitrary choice within the sales-magicians universe, pay your money-energy and probably feel good about your choice.

It is reasonable in this reality to have limits and limited choices. Without limits, reality becomes chaotic and sometimes may become frightening for those who cannot understand what is happening.

When we can tolerate uncertainty and chaos we have more options as well as more pain and disappointment. One of the underlying reasons for trance is to eliminate part of the global awareness and to reduce the chaos to a more reasonable and less complicated set of choices. Trance helps to reduce the chaos that is attached to variety.

Trance is the mental condition which makes it reasonable to accept limited choices. Trance restricts primitive chaos or chlinthonic energy and helps us to harness that energy in the same way that a salesman harnesses our money energy in order to create a sale. In restraining the chaos, energy may be focused into the creation. Trance, therefore, has something to do with energy utilization and the potentiation of creation. This is an important point.

It is important to study trance in order to understand how we may increase the awareness of our options while we are in many inevitable trances, and, at the same time, to understand the inherent limitations of trance as a process to defeat ignorance. Trance is a two-edged sword: it allows us to focus our awareness, enabling us to accomplish many wonderful things, and on the other hand it inhibits broad awareness, disabling choice. It is important to understand that trances in life are as common as grains of sand and more numerous.

The study of trance is also esoteric. That is, there is a component of the knowledge of trance that is hidden. It is one part of the nature of trance itself to hide and to be esoteric.

One natural boundary of trance divides awareness into the conscious and the unconscious. This is one reason trance is esoteric.

The division between the conscious and the unconscious is the most scary division of all. We know about one but not about the other. At the root of this fear is the fear of death; it is the fear of the loss of the ego, and the submergence of the "I" into the primordial chaos. What I hope to show in this book is that if you can understand how trance works, then you have the possibility to penetrate this veil between the conscious and the unconscious in a certain way. That is, there is a technique of both losing the ego and regaining it again.

A Scientific Point of View

I realize that my definition of trance, as it evolved from my personal experiences, may differ from definitions that are more usual, so I want to review the subject at some length here.

The word *trance* is popularly thought of as describing an unusual state of mind. Trance is usually understood to be an *altered* state of consciousness, and not the normal one. And the word *trance* is often associated with the word *hypnosis*. Both words have negative connotations in the sense that they imply a loss of conscious individual will. The negative connotations may lead most people to be unaware of the extent to which trance exists in all areas of life. Even more important, trance techniques can and are used in advertising and social control. Don't you think it is time you learned to identify those techniques that others use to take away your conscious choice? Making you aware of these techniques is one main purpose of this book.

Gilligan (1987) sees the trance condition as biologically

essential for all human beings. He says that trance is experienced in daydreaming, dancing, listening to music, reading a book, watching television, and can be induced through rhythmic and repetitive movement (dancing, running, breathing exercises, etc.), through chanting, meditation, prayer, group rituals, etc.; by focusing attention on an image, an idea, the sound of someone's voice; through relaxation, massage, warm baths, etc.; and through drugs such as alcohol, cannabis, or tranquilizers.

Altered states of consciousness is a term used to describe all kinds of mental states. The term became necessary perhaps because so many people were taking drugs, doing meditation, practicing hypnosis and magic. Modern communication — TV especially — made people aware that there were yogis in India and witch doctors in South American jungles who each had their ways of entering an altered state or trance. The term altered state was an attempt to circumscribe these special mental phenomena in order to have a more well-defined area for scientific research. According to most modern classifications, a trance is a type of altered state. But I believe that so many terms only tend to confuse what is really going on.

I believe that we are more in various trance states than not. To me trance is a relatively common mental state and there appears to be a continuum from what may be called *normal thinking* to intense, deep and extraordinary trance states.

Because the nature of such a continuum has not been well defined, there has been considerable confusion over the last 200 years as to what a trance is, what hypnosis is, what meditation is, and what addiction is. It is as though arbitrary boundaries of consciousness were to be constructed which would somehow enable people to say: "That's a trance; that's only hypnosis and these are all altered states of consciousness." One current scientific view, for example, is that hypnosis does not really exist, and it is grouped in the same category as leprechauns and witchcraft; that is, a belief structure which presumably can be explained by other well-known processes.

This 'skeptical' conception of hypnosis was proposed by Theodore Sarbin in 1950 as a social-psychological alternative to both the Paris and the Nancy schools of thought about the nature of hypnosis. This skeptical conception continues to be a subject in academic circles; as recently as 1992 Wagstaff suggested that it would be better to disregard all the standard references to trance or altered states and to stick with explanations from a social and psychological perspective. If psychologists were convinced that they must abandon the term, perhaps that is one reason that "trance" is now a musical genre.

Historically, a *trance* was the term that was used to describe certain states that yogis, spiritualist mediums or channellers might go into in order to perform their particularly extraordinary behaviors.

Mostly, one associates trance with some type of hypnotic state of mind, and I will need to explore both hypnosis and trance in some detail before describing my own ideas, primarily because hypnosis and trance are seemingly so closely related, and there are so many popular misconceptions as to what hypnosis is or is not.

Trance and hypnosis are commonly associated terms. *Trance* is also the term used by certain spiritualist mediums and yogis in describing meditation states and other phenomena that psychologist might refer to as 'dissociative' because something about the personality of a person in a trance appears to be split off from the usual response patterns.

One researcher in hypnotic phenomena, Orne, discovered that there are unique characteristics exhibited by a person in a trance. Orne made this observation from highly consistent verbal reports of hypnotized subjects and from various clinical and empirical studies. Orne called this alteration of function *trance logic*. Trance logic refers to a set of characteristics of mental functions that are specifically found in deep trance as opposed to light trance.

Trance logic includes an alteration in language processing as well as a decrease in critical judgement of language processing and in increased tolerance for incongruity as well as interpreting words much more literally.

Besides the 'skeptical' school of thought which believes trance phenomena can be adequately explained by the social psychological concepts of belief and compliance, there are other theories of trance that propose that trance generally represents some kind of psychological regression to an earlier developmental state, or that trance is 'contact with the unconscious mind' or that deep trance is somehow a selective use of one hemisphere of the brain. Some psychologists (Janet and later Hilgard) would characterize a trance as a dissociative state because the personality appears to be distinct from the usual or normal one and this perception has given rise to the cognitive dissociation theory. The theory of the 'Fantasy Prone Personality' of T. X. Barber and his colleague Sheryl Wilson suggests loose correlates between naturally visionary individuals with a rich inner life, and with the natural capacity to produce extraordinary psychosomatic responses, yet who are perfectly able to distinguish their vivid fantasy life from reality, and who exhibit pronounced hypnotizability and various psychic abilities.

Although classic hypnosis research has demonstrated that

people respond differently to suggestions under different conditions, a lack of a model for trance is probably responsible for the fact that relatively little work has been done to determine the precise details of how each suggestion effect occurs.

When a phenomena such as trance lacks a model to explain what it is and how it works, people are free to make up stories and to impute a magic, a mystery and a fear to trance phenomena which is totally unnecessary. The magic and mystery of trance is exciting, but fear and ignorance of it gives power equally to both the healers as well as to the unscrupulous who can exploit the entranced to their own profit.

Common and Uncommon Trances

Our Unconscious Trance States

Are you aware that you are in a light trance as you read these words? Most people slip in and out of various kinds of trance states hundreds of times during what is called the *normal waking state*. Trance is a special type of dissociation that helps us to organize and process information automatically. You would not be able to really understand the written print marks on this page unless there existed other types of mental processing going on which organized the written patterns and linked them to prior memories or associations. These other mental processing activities are happening unconsciously right now. Some people would say that this unconscious process is another type of awareness. Gurdjieff taught that to become aware that you are asleep is the first step in waking up. If you are interested in being able to modify these unconscious mental processes, it is essential to become aware of the trances you are in; in fact, in some sense you can count your trances. Making you aware of what some of these unconscious processes are and how they got there and how they can be modified is one purpose of this book.

There are good trances and bad trances. There are light trances, deep trances, short-term trances and lifelong trances. There are pain relieving trances and pain producing trances. There are healing trances and pathological trances. These are just a few areas where common trances can be found: hypnosis, music, TV, meditation, addictions, religions and work.

So what is a *trance*? To many psychologists a *trance* is a state of limited awareness. Some psychologists would also characterize trance as a form of sleep, or dreamlike awareness or a kind of altered state of consciousness. Certainly trance has long been associated with hypnotic states, and with the altered states of consciousness of dervishes, shamans and yogis. Meditation does produce strong trance states. However, in my opinion, trance states are much more common than is normally believed. We can also count daydreaming as a trance, as well as watching movies or television. Many relationships with people seem to have trancelike qualities: love relationships, power relationships, relationships with charismatic people, relationships with gurus, shamans and so on. Coming into contact with drug addicts or psychotics often seems to invoke strange trance states.

For many decades, trance has been associated with parapsychological experiences. According to William James and other researchers, a Mrs. Piper — an ordinary woman in most circumstances — could enter into a trance and give information that was both accurate and which she could not have ordinarily discovered. For example, once, when a stranger visited her for the first time, she went into a trance and described his dead father, saying many correct things, such as the fact that he had a bald spot where men are not usually bald, on the right side of the head. She pointed to that place and the stranger said that an accident had indeed made his father bald, asymmetrically, at that spot. Mrs. Piper also told the stranger many other accurate and uncommon details, such as the pet name which only his father had used for him, and the way in which his half-brother died (Hodgson).

Laubscher, an anthropologist, tested a South African diviner reputed to have marvelous abilities. Laubscher went to a deserted place, checked that no one was within his vision, took a purse wrapped in brown paper, buried it, put a brown stone above it and a gray stone above that. Then he got into his car and drove as fast as he could 60 miles to where the diviner lived. He asked the diviner what he had done. The diviner began to perform a seance dance. After some time, he described the purse, the brown paper it was wrapped it, and precise, accurate details of both the brown stone and the gray stone. There are many other cases which have indicated the existence of a connection of trance with parapsychological phenomena.

In America, psychic healers are likely to prepare for healing by meditation or prayer; in many parts of Africa, preparation for psychic healing involves a prolonged ritual dance. Dervishes twirl.

If the unusual trance state of a shaman or a yogi is desirable, then we might be tempted to believe that all trance states are desirable states. What might distinguish the trance of a yogi from the trance of a drug addict? What is the difference between a television trance and the trance that we experience when daydreaming? It is possible to enter into trances which relieve pain, such as when going to a dentist who uses hypnosis to produce anesthesia.

If compulsive drinking or eating could be shown to be trances, an argument could be made that trance can produce involuntary self-destructive behavior and therefore a model for trance might indicate ways to control such behaviors.

Hypnotic Trances

The type of trance studied most has been the hypnotic trance. Milton Erickson, the great psychotherapist, had wonderful and nearly immediate psychological cures in a great many of his patients. His technique was called "Ericksonian hypnosis." Many people tried to explain what it was that he did, because in many cases, his patients claimed that they were not hypnotized and they were not in any kind of trance at all. Erickson's recorded dialogs were analyzed for years to try to find out what it was exactly that made his form of hypnotherapy so successful.

Richard Bandler, John Grinder and others were successful in finally analyzing and modelling Erickson's techniques. They devised what they called "neuro-linguistic programming," also known as NLP, which is based primarily on Erickson's techniques. With NLP it is relatively easy to hypnotize a person and to keep that person in a trance state without their being aware that they are in fact in a trance. The technique of pacing and leading a subject from a rich or varied set of thoughts to a limited, internal and impoverished set of thoughts is a well-known technique used consciously by hypnotists, advertisers, sales people, preachers and politicians.

Many stage hypnotists use Ericksonian or NLP derived hypnotic techniques in order to induce trance. TV hypnotists on daytime television can induce a trance after only a few minutes of seemingly innocuous talk. During this time, the subject can be given posthypnotic suggestions to alter behavior and perception in peculiar ways during the TV show. Stage hypnotists often have dramatic shows in which peculiar and unusual physiological powers can be demonstrated.

Television advertisers and the designers of commercials are aware of the techniques of Bandler and Grinder and use them often in commercials. For example, commercials will often attempt to invoke past memories and in doing so effectively associate pleasant or strong memories with their products. Cigarette and liquor ads are especially keen to use these types of associations, and, in essence, they abuse the consumer by promoting the connection of healthy associations with their products. The trance-induction potential of television media is well-known and is often used for manipulating consumer tastes. It should be no surprise that political candidates know they must be able to successfully use the hypnotic power of television in order to win elections. However useful television is for commercial and social control reasons, it cannot be reasonably argued that using trance in order to promote a political agenda, is in the end, really socially beneficial.

Salespersons, preachers and politicians are aware of ordinary hypnotic techniques and often consciously use NLP or Ericksonian techniques in order to promote their own agendas. As you talk with a salesperson or listen to a preacher or politician on television you might never admit that you were in a trance of any kind. Have you ever spaced out listening to a preacher? Politicians? Computer software salespersons? Then you'd better learn more about trance.

Some professional sales training institutes unabashedly teach hypnotic techniques to their sales trainees. It is clear to them that if a buyer is put into a hypnotic trance then it is much easier to sell a product. And this is true, but only because the buyer's critical judgement is disabled. Because the ethics of using such techniques on the unaware is questionable, some states, like California, have laws that give you the right to cancel major contracts within 24 or 48 hours of signing. Supposedly, this gives you enough time to "wake up" from your unconscious state. The law is silent, however, on unwritten or casual commercial contracts.

So how can you tell if you are in one of these ordinary, unconscious trances? You are in a trance when your attention is limited and there is a certain repetition of thoughts. In an extreme case, your attention is so limited that it feels like "tunnel vision." The repetition of thoughts might be mantras, songs, repeating fantasies, or even the math calculations of balancing your checkbook before you make that purchase. That song you can't get out of your head indicates a trance. Concentration, when the mind is focused on a specific problem or thought, is also a form of trance. You could characterize the fundamental nature of trance cybernetically as an awareness *loop*, or a circular flow of consciousness.

This looping, or circular flow of consciousness, is well-known as a mechanism for inducing trance. The repetition of mantras, the whirling of dervishes, the chanting and drumming of shamans, the repetition of TV commercials all induce different trances by limiting your attention and overloading your mind with repeated thoughts. The purposes may be different, the results may be different, but in my opinion the difference in the resulting trance is mainly of degree.

From a systems analytical point of view, the looping of awareness is easy to describe and seems to be at the cause of a wide variety of trances. In my own personal experience it appears that the looping alone is the necessary and sufficient condition to induce a dissociated condition. Taking the looping as the singular cause of trance seems to offer an explanation of a wide variety of trancelike phenomena. In addition, this singular condition groups a wide variety of phenomena into the definition as trance or trancelike phenomena. Once this genera of trance or trancelike phenomena has been circumscribed, then it remains to denote the differentia and conditions.

Whether you are passively watching TV football, or engaging in rational rigorously precise thoughts, or having an emotional jolt of religious fervor, or feeling patriotic passion, or if you are an addict of any kind, or if you have the compassionless mindset of a mass murderer you are in a trance. Why? Because all these states encourage a fixed, narrow attention span and they all reward the repetition of an impoverished set of thoughts. It is important to identify all of these states as trance because they all promote a limitation of attention. Because of this limiting of attention, trance creates unaware-ness or a "sleeping state" in those areas of life where the attention is absent. Because the thoughts are repeating, the limiting of attention becomes fixed, and can therefore alter perception. That is, new information might not be processed correctly. For example, if the repeating thought is "everything I see is blue," and the eyes are shown a red object, then eventually the repeated idea in the mind will make the object seem blue and it will be believed to be blue; and red will not be seen or if seen, not believed as really red. Brainwashing and propaganda techniques use the fact that the repetition of a thought can result in its eventual acceptance. Many types of trances, but not all, promote a singlemindedness which can become self-destructive. Some of these trances could be described as pathological.

The genera of trance must include a wide variety of trances, some of which are manifestly pathological and others which add a richness to life and which can be appreciated as spectacular or magical. What characterizes this differentia? What are the conditions for a pathological trance, under this definition?

Many types of trances, of course, are not pathological. Such trances are used to enhance creativity, relation, problem solving, altering sensations, altering perception, creating pleasure, humor, enhancing delicate and subtle understanding, to find new ways to understand experience, to perceive old things in new ways, to have new pleasures in life, to create the courage to change relationships and in the personal mystery of life itself. These non-pathological trances also are created through the narrowing of attention, and the repetition of thoughts to create personal power.

It is well-known that the skillful use of trance, whether hypnotic or meditation, can increase telepathic sensitivities and other abilities. Janet, a highly respected psychiatrist and researcher in the early days of hypnosis, reported extraordinary telepathic success with hypnosis. Dukhan & Rao tested dozens of students of a guru in India for psi. They found that postmeditation the student scored significantly higher in psi-hitting than in the premeditation control tests. There have been many other researchers reporting similar findings over decades.

One of the important effects of a normal trance is to temporarily decrease body awareness and to temporarily disable memory. With less awareness of the body and of the past, there is an increase in creative potential. Latent problem solving skills may come into existence easier when the limitations of the body and memory are disabled. Short-term trance states are occasionally desirable to increase creativity and problem solving potentials.

What many people call concentration is actually a trance. When the mind is concentrated on understanding something new or solving a difficult problem it may momentarily become dissociated and allow an increase in creative problem solving skills.

Participatory sports such as basketball, football, swimming and so on, require that the participant repeat movements. The repetition of these movements combined with the limiting of attention required by the rules of the particular sport or skill would probably produce trance. In most cases, the trance will cause both a decrease of body awareness and allow for problem solving skills to emerge. It is these secondary effects of natural trance which may partially underlie the popularity of sports in general and to give the impression that sports help to create valuable but nonspecific skills.

Computer games can also be used to produce trances. Computer games are interactive, and that means that they narrow the attention and feed back stimulation to the player which engages their attention even more. When players are in the types of trances that a computer game produces, the players become susceptible to hypnotic suggestions.

In some computer games, for example *Endorfun* by Time Warner, subliminal messages can be introduced to lure players into trance states. Subliminal messages such as "I expect pleasure and satisfaction," and "It's okay for me to have everything I want", however, can lead players into addictive states. That is, players who may be unhappy or angry or frustrated in life could become psychologically dependent on the positive strokes of some subliminal messages. On the other hand, subliminal messages, such as the above, promoting unrealistic expectations will eventually only produce disappointment, frustration and anger. Is this simply bad trance engineering or is it deliberate trance abuse?

Under the 1990 Broadcasting Act, television and radio companies cannot produce programs or advertisements that exploit the possibility of "influencing the minds of persons watching without them being fully aware of what has occurred." However, no such legislation exists to regulate the computer industry. It is not the computer or any media, however, that is at fault; it is the willful exploitation of an induced trance.

Once the mechanics of trance induction become well-known, it may be that a reading of the 1990 Broadcasting Act would include even the choice of words used by actors in a sitcom inasmuch as such scripts — when written hypnotically — may be used to influence social, commercial and political beliefs. Even direct mail advertising received in your mailbox contains hypnotically written scripts. Are you aware of this?

It is also well-known that when you are in a trance your attention can be diverted effectively enough to produce anesthesia sufficient for dental work or some types of surgery. Lamaze natural childbirth breathing techniques uses the resulting narrowed span of attention to help reduce pain. This narrowing of attention, the concentration of the mind on maintaining the breathing patterns, diverts the attention from the physical pain sensations during childbirth with the result that the mother becomes less aware of any uncomfortable sensations. The power of a mind in a trance can do things which it ordinarily cannot do. Giving birth painlessly is only one example. Conscious control of breathing patterns is used by yogis, as pranayama, for example, in order to influence the mind or to induce altered states.

Trance can also be used to reduce psychological pain such as anxiety, fear, worry, as well as the universal *Weltschmerz.* Instead of consciously addressing the causes of the pain, trance can successfully divert the attention so that one is aware of neither the pain nor of the causes of pain. While the use of trance for specific instances of analgesia may be beneficial for surgery or in emergency situations, the use of trance to avoid situations of a long-term or permanent duration impoverishes life and prevents new possibilities. It is the use of trance in this latter sense which makes trance into a form of addiction.

Hypnotic trance is only one way to remove pain. Alcohol, drug, religion, work, consumption, and TV trance addictions can also be counted as other ways of removing pain. I believe addictions of all sorts are forms of pathological trances a central purpose of which is pain control.

If trance is defined as fixed or limited thinking, then nearly all human activities create some type of trance. The bounded circles of thinking that keep us in trances are countless. The entire "ordered universe" is a trance. But there is an escapists pleasure in remaining in trance and a deep human fear of the chaos which can result if there were no trance "order" to life.

Socialization itself is the process of putting a person into a long-term trance. You do not go to work naked because of socialization. The socialization process started by parents and continued by religious training, schools, universities, the military and employment in different ways all create a multiplicity of long-term trance-states, the result of which puts you in a bounded circle of limited but socially and culturally acceptable activity. Without these long-term trances life would be more chaotic and perhaps you would be more painfully aware of too many choices. Every choice we make limits our options and makes life seem more manageable. When we stick to our choices at all costs we are in a pathological trance.

By becoming aware that we are in these trances, we may begin to realize that we can also change them in more creative ways. It is as Gurdieff said: to wake up, we must become aware that we are asleep.

Religious Trance

The practice of religion for millennia has involved the practice of trance and used a variety of trance-inducing activity. Prayer, meditation, chanting all will induce trance. The effect of trance when taken to extremes and in the hands of experts can produce many magical effects, including the healing of the body, knowledge of secrets, the discovery of hidden knowledge, knowledge of the future, as well as having an influence on the weather, on social beliefs and on the outcome of war. In addition, religious trance can produce an easy tolerance and acceptance for many of life's inevitable disappointments.

There are religious healers who, by means of their special meditative trances, can perform spectacular healings — including psychic surgery — on others. Such healers may certainly be envied for these powers. Yet, unfortunately, even the meditative trances conducted from the altrusistic motivations of a pious devotion to a God or Goddess can become pathological if they become an end in themselves. By knowing how to identify pathological trances as well as how they are created it is possible to avoid them.

Faith, or belief in a set of ideas or paradigms without evidence, often indicates, unfortunately, faulty judgement, faulty memory, and possibly hallucinations. Since these are characteristics of trance, the profession of a faith or belief can presumably be traced to a repetition of limited ideas and the resulting dissociative trance.

In general, it can be said that faith and belief are indicative of trances in which a reduction of emotional pain awareness is the goal. I would be surprised if the profession of faith and belief did not hide a hidden depression for which an addictive trance state is ameliorating.

Religions which encourage and promote personal demonstrations of faith and belief often are attempting to create similar conditions that might be associated with a single-minded devotion to God, but very often what is really produced seems to be very much like an addiction. Addictions do produce deep trances and trances with relatively stabile characteristics. But, however seemingly powerful the addictive trances are, and how convincingly it may appear that those in religious addictive trances are extremely devoted and singleminded towards their guru, God or Goddess, the nature of an addictive trance is always self-delusion, deception and destruction.

Charismatic religious leaders often have stabile trances and such stabile trances can affect people who come into their sphere of influence as though they had magical powers or had tapped into powerful energies of an unknown type. These energies or magical powers are generated by trance. They have similarities to addictive trances but different in an important but subtle way. The trance model which I describe in the following pages shows these differences.

A Suggested Model for Trance

Introduction

The field is open for nearly anyone to propose a theory of hypnosis. If the real work of science begins once a community of workers has adopted a unified theoretical paradigm (Kuhn, 1962), then, arguably, the real work of the science of hypnosis has not yet *properly* begun. So long as there is no unified theoretical paradigm the reality of hypnotic states is put into question (Wagstaff, 1991). Wagstaff also argues for the need of a change in terminology.

At present, there seem to be two major schools of thought on the nature of hypnosis: the neodissociative, and the social-psychological. The neodissociative model differs from the social psychological model in that it is a systems model and does not assume a "purpose" to hypnotically suggested behavior.

McClelland and Rumelhart (1986) recognize that thinking and problem solving are a result of what they call "parallel distributed processing". Hilgard too suggests parallel processing as a useful concept (Stava & Jaffa, 1988).

I have a simple model for trance which uses the idea of parallel distributed processing, but in such a way that may be used in a systems or in an automated measurement environment. I will rephrase some current problems in hypnotic theory, describe some pathological trance conditions and some possible therapeutic intervention strategies. The idea is not to replace therapists with computer systems, but to explore the theoretical implications of such a paradigm. The implications of the trance model suggest practical applications in research and in therapy.

It is obvious that human cognition does not function the same as an electronic parallel distributed processor. However, limitations in adapting information systems theory to human cognition may depend partly on the fact that at present there is no reliable way to detect the presence of a discrete thought in a specific individual at a specific time. If there were such a technique then the following theoretical model might also be useful in an experimental context.

Trances, as defined by this model, are not difficult to produce. In fact, by this definition trances are quite common. Strong, spectacular and long-lasting trances have popularized the false notion that all trances are special states. The model implies that spectacular trances can be produced through the modification of specific conditions that produce trance. The strength of a trance can be objectively measured by using this model. In the future, the application of the principles described by the model may enable the researcher or therapist to design trances for specific purposes and to objectively measure the results.

Elements of Thought

At this point I will not define 'thoughts', but merely note that they exist. To gain maximum scope, I will use the word thought to include feeling as well. As I develop the model, a more complete definition for thought may emerge. The reason for this approach is that without a system framework already in place a definition of thought would be premature. However, we can make some general observations.

We know that when we are awake we have thoughts. We know that we think about whatever it is that is important to us.

If something is very important, we will think about it more often than if it is not important to us. We may not know what is absolutely important, and, for many reasons, we might not think at all about what is truly vital. Whether important or not, true or not, vital or not, our thoughts repeat.

I think no one has ever counted their thoughts, but we can assume that a specific thought will repeat a countable number of times over a specific time period. For example, the thought that is symbolized by *mother* may repeat 156,792 times over a period of a lifetime. On the other hand, the thought that is symbolized by *father* may repeat only 14 times over the period of time from 7:16 am Sunday until 16:45 Monday.

Why count thoughts when they seem to spring to consciousness and then disappear entirely as if obeying unknown forces? Why count specific thoughts if they have such a short life and spring from such a deep and dark well? Why count them if they are a part of a complex sequence, and have their own unknowable agendas? Ephemeral thoughts have no weight or mass, and taken out of context, they may seem to be of very little importance.

There is also the problem of measuring thoughts. Although it is obvious that we have distinct thoughts, it is not yet possible to count them reliably. We cannot say with certainty that any given person had an extraordinary number of thoughts about "chickens" or "Jesus" and what an extraordinary number of thoughts might mean. On the other hand, there is no reliable mechanism known at present to be able to say that any given person "never thought about Zanzibar."

Thoughts are also difficult to categorize. What does it mean to think the word "hair," for example? The multiple associations of a word, its dependency on its changing contexts as well as the subjective conditions, all make measurement and categorization difficult.

Thoughts, Thought Objects and Brain Waves

As it functions the brain generates minute electrical charges. Presumably, these minute electrical charges represent some of the components of thoughts or bear some relationship with what we subjectively experience as thought objects or states of awareness. These electrical charges form a variety of waves which have been identified as follows:

Beta Waves

Beta waves are the most common of the brain wave patterns that occur when awake. These occur during period of intense concentration, problem solving, and focused analysis. The frequency of beta waves is between 13-30 Hz (cycles per second).

Alpha Waves

Alpha waves are most common when we are mentally alert, calm and relaxed, or when day-dreaming. The frequency of alpha waves is between 8-12 Hz.

Theta Waves

Theta waves occur when we are mentally drowsy and unfocused, during deep calmness or relaxation, as for example we make the transitions from drowsiness to sleep or from sleep to the waking state. The frequency of theta waves is between 4-7 Hz.

Delta Waves

Delta waves occur primarily during deep sleep or states of unconsciousness. The frequency of delta waves is between 0.5-4 Hz.

Brain Wave Synchronization and the Frequency Following Effect

2000 years ago Ptolemy and Apuleius noted that differing rates of flickering lights had an effect on states of awareness and on the production of epilepsy. In the late 1920s it was discovered that when light was played on the closed eyelids an echoing production of brain wave frequencies was produced. In 1965 Grey used a stroboscope to send rhythmic light flashes into the eyes at a rate of from 10-25 Hz. He discovered that this stimulated similar brain wave activity.

More recent research by Budzynski, Oestrander and others, in the use of brain machines suggest that photic or direct electrical stimulation of the brain in the theta range appears to facilitate rapid learning, produce deep relaxation, euphoria, an increase in creativity, problem solving ability and is apparently associated with enhanced concentration and accelerated learning.

It seems as though there is a mechanism in which the repeated stimulation can produce effects which are also demonstrated by trance.

Measuring Thoughts

It is not yet possible to measure with both precision and accuracy, the occurrence of a specific thought in a specific person at a specific time. However, recent research at Yale University with functional magnetic resonance imaging, or fast MRI, is demonstrating the possibility of locating where in the human brain, cell activity is greatest for specific stimulations. Fast MRI or other advanced techniques may in the future enable researchers to measure thoughts.

New technologies such as computerized electroencephalographic (EEG) frequency analysis, EEG topographic brain mapping, positron emission tomography, regional cerebral blood flow, single photon emission computed tomography and nuclear magnetic resonance imaging allow more sophistication to be used in the ongoing investigation of the neurophysiological processes of cognitive functioning. A specific thought may or may not contribute sufficient energy to allow detection by one or more of the instruments above. However, a power map study of fractal dimensional analysis of EEG conducted recently at the Institute of Hypnosis in Tokyo, seems to indicate that the discrete measurement of physiological changes of awareness is possible (Kawano, 1995).

It seems as if there are three current directions of inquiry: the neurophysiological, the social-psychological and the cognitive behaviorialist. The neurophysiological approach does not yet have a mapping from physiological measurements to human thought. The social-psychological approach can measure the gross subjective and social effects of thoughts but this approach seems to lack precision and provoke controversy. Cognitive behaviorialists apparently use systems concepts and analytical techniques, but until now, trance seems not to be a subject for them.

One researcher in trance, Orne (1959), concluded that objective correlates to the hypnotic condition were not to be found in available physiological measurements. Orne concluded that he would have to use verbal reports of subjective experience rather than rely on objective measurements. Orne's conclusions seem to have led many current researchers to base much of their research on the subjective reports of hypnotic subjects. Perhaps the lack of the development of a hypnotic or trance theory which has not been based on Orne's assumptions is due to the fact that physiological measurements of thoughts simply do not exist at this time, nor did they exist when Orne made his conclusions.

If thoughts are based on our senses and on the processes of physical organs, it may be argued that our thoughts have their roots in the muck and ooze of digestion, reproduction, circulation and respiration; and, although these chlinthonian processes are cyclical, none of them are regular, nor are any of these processes fully understood. What was perhaps easier for research psychologists — although finally less precise — was to turn away from the physical foundations of cognition and to deal with more palatable and abstract concepts based on social and psychological models.

Our thoughts are fundamentally based on our health and the quality of the energy which is available for mentation. Our thoughts are indirectly influenced by environmental mechanisms that are not yet fully recognized nor understood. Our thoughts are dependent on factors which are not easy to measure and not easy to describe. When awareness is low or more like an animal, our thoughts may be more easily correlated to a variety of physiological causes. But, when awareness is high or abstract, our thoughts seem to take paths which are not directly derived from physiological causes alone.

Yet, sequences of thoughts form to make sentences and sentences form to make concepts. Bodies of concepts are the building blocks of abstract knowledge. Thoughts as feelings underlay the social fabric and drive relationships. It is the patterns of sequences of thoughts that are important, and repeated patterns give a weighted importance through their natural occurrence.

In this model, thoughts are not only words or sentences; thoughts may be nonverbal, visual, sensual, tactile, abstract, auditory, etc. Cognitive behavioralists call these *thought objects.* The basic idea of the model is to be specific as to the physiological foundations of thought for measurement purposes and to redefine explicitly the relatively abstract terms of psychology. This leaves room for the possibility that specific thoughts will one day be measured and that the results of these measurements will be processed by computers. The model's theoretical concepts assume the objective mensuration of thought must be defined in such a way that there is no room for ambiguity.

The Model

Definitions

Throughout this article the following symbols are used.

s is used to specify a thought sequence of an arbitrary length.

e is used to specify the awareness of s.

c is used to specify a closed loop of thoughts. In general, c is a repeating subset of s.

d is the collective latent awareness that is created by c. d is also referred as the *dissociated trance plane* (sometimes referred to as the DTP) of c.

Subscripts on these symbols are meant to denote specific instances of them.

Thoughts

As used here, *s* denotes a thought or thought object which can be uniquely described by a set of physiological measurements. Subscripts on s, such as s_1, s_2, etc. denote a specific sequence of thoughts which occur sequentially in relative increasing time order without specifying the time interval. A specific sequence of thoughts may be denoted such as $S = (s_1, s_2, ..., s_k)$.

Every person knows what he or she thinks. But not a single person can record every thought as it occurs. Symbols, such as words, or sentences, can be recorded. Pictures can be painted which may represent a group of thoughts, but the thoughts themselves cannot be painted. One might imagine that a poem or a stream of consciousness utterance or a word salad more accurately represents thoughts as they occur, but it is more likely that such represented thoughts are only a subsequence of the actual recorded thoughts.

Energy and Awareness

We assume that there is an attenuation of the awareness of a thought during the transition to its successor and that attenuation occurs for physical energy conservation reasons. While awareness is wholly dependent on the physical energy available for cognition, the model separates what may be termed raw cognitive energy from an awareness which is bound to a specific thought.

e denotes a measure of an individual's awareness of a thought. e is a set of measurements that uniquely describes a measurable physiological condition, not a subjective report. The awareness e_1 is greatest when the energy of consciousness is at s_1, but it should also be possible to measure the residual awareness e_1 when consciousness is at s_2. I will denote this second measurement $e_1(s_2)$, and note the identity, $e_i(s_i) = e_i$. What this means is that when we think thoughts, the thoughts don't last. They naturally fade away. The fading away of a thought as awareness transits from one thought to another follows an attenuation function.

Transitions from one thought, s_a to another, s_b, occur when $e_b > e_a(s_b)$, by definition. One important measurement is the average transition value e_g which occurs when $e_b > e_g > e_a(s_b)$. e_g is not a constant value. Thoughts fade away or become "unconscious" depending on some physiological values which are always changing. e_g is that point of awareness when one thought changes into another.

We assume that there is an attenuation of the awareness of a thought s_1 during the transition of awareness to its successor s_2. This attenuation results in predecessor thoughts becoming latent specifically when $e_1(s_2) < e_g$. When we have a new thought, we forget about the old thought.

Attenuation of a thought at $e_1(s_2) < e_g$ does not necessarily imply that $e_1(s_2)$ is an "unconscious" state. We can sometimes, under some conditions, keep old thoughts in our heads as well as new thoughts.

Thresholds, Conditions and States

We now consider what is meant by a state of awareness K. Whenever e is within a defined set range of values, $K_1 < e < K_2$, there are associated two *thresholds* of awareness, K_1 and K_2, or *conditions* of awareness, $K_1 < e$, and $e < K_2$. Within these awareness condition boundary thresholds, an individuals awareness is described as being in a specific *state of awareness*.

Another way to look at K is as a set of measurable enabling or disabling physiological conditions. For example, K may be a limit in which e is disabled for critical thinking and enabled for hallucination. Such a value for K would circumscribe states of awareness in which "trance logic" would also be found.

Note that while e is defined as a multidimensional vector of unknown dimension, the thresholds K are also sets of values. The conditions "less than" and "greater than" are not operations on scalars, but on the multidimensional vector e, so conditions should be interpreted so as to unambiguously place e either within or outside a corresponding threshold range.

In the normal awakened condition, we do have thoughts. If we could record them all, we would discover one long fuzzy sequence of them starting, perhaps, at birth, and ending, perhaps, at death. We would be awake during only some portions of this long thought sequence. Other portions we would not. If our awareness threshold at birth is K_α and our awareness threshold at death is K_ω, and we focus only on thoughts that we have during the awake condition, K_β, of consciousness, then the sequence of thoughts within the awareness interval (K_α, K_ω), would appear to be discontinuous.

However, within the continuous awareness interval (K_α, K_ω) are a multiple set of awareness states which are interesting to researchers. We can list some of them grossly: awake, sleep, dreaming, altered state of consciousness (ASC), trance, etc. but these terms are not sufficiently defined at present to be able to discriminate between adjacent states with both precision and accuracy. (Tart, 1992) It would be helpful to know precisely which physiological measurements comprise the components of a vector e with the smallest dimensions, such that a set of conditions of discrimination, K, would unambiguously define a specific state of awareness.

Thought Sequences

If s_1 is a thought, then the next thought we might have, s_2, is somehow connected with s_1. Presumably, s_2 will be followed by a further sequence of thoughts, s_3, ..., s_k, until, at last, we are overcome with sleep. At that point, we hypothesize that an awareness threshold, K_s, has been breached, and that s_{k+1}, ..., s_m, are thoughts that we may have when our awareness is outside threshold K_s, that is, when we are asleep.

Awareness thresholds are multidimensional and at present imprecisely defined. For example, it is not known precisely what "sleep" is, nor what ASC one is in when one seems to be "asleep." For example, if one active thought process $e_i(s_i)$ > K_s while at the same time another active thought process $e_j(s_j)$ < K_s, is one unconscious, hypnotized, dreaming, asleep or in an ASC? The answer would depend on how the K values of each state are defined. The general social-psychological abstractions for ASCs are currently too imprecisely defined to be used in a model for trance. What is implied is that terms denoting so-called *states of consciousness* are arbitrarily defined based on their relative occurrence. Such arbitrary definitions imply social and cultural factors determine what "unconscious" is.

Our thoughts repeat. We have similar experiences from day to day and most of us with a memory seem to learn something from our experiences. Learning presumes the existence of memory.

If we take this singular long sequence of thoughts, and collect all the thoughts that are the same, we will find several different patterns, some of which are above some arbitrary threshold of an aware condition and others will be below that same threshold of awareness.

For example, taking words as thoughts, if we could collect all instances that a person thought the word "home" we would find that some words would precede "home" and other words would follow "home". If we counted these words which preceded or followed "home" we could arbitrarily group the words with high counts as "consciously associated" and the words with relatively low counts as "unconsciously associated," thereby transforming a condition of association into an arbitrary category of a state of consciousness.

Associations

When we think, then our awareness goes from one thought to another. Another way to look at this is to say that one thought is *associated* with another.

If we assume a probabilistic model for an association function, we could say that the probability that s_i would be followed by s_j is $p_i(s_i)$. Although probabilistic models lose information, association linkages based on probabilistic models (Wier, 1967) or machines which use fuzzy logic can successfully simulate human behavior to some degree only to the extent that a condition of association corresponds reliably to a category of an arbitrary state of consciousness.

Hebb's learning law, "Let us assume then that the persistence or repetition of a reverberatory activity (or *trace*) tends to induce lasting cellular changes that add to its stability ... When an axon of cell A is near enough to excite a cell B and repeatedly or persistently takes part in firing it, some growth process or metabolic change takes place in one or both cells such that A's efficiency, as on of the cells firing B, increased" implies a physiological basis for association.

Channels

The set of potentially associated thoughts and their probabilities for which $p_x > 0$ represents the *channel* for s_x. Channels may be narrow in the case of a few x, or under conditions which restrict choice. For a given thought there is a domain of possible associations.

Going the other way from s_x, there is a set of thoughts, s_a, ..., s_b, for which s_x is the *pattern*; that is, the range of specific thoughts which have the same domain of possible associations.

While a singular thought is of some interest because it is the foundation of our discussion, it is not as interesting as the regular association of thoughts we know as patterns.

From the point of view of trance, the patterns of a thought may be used to trigger or evoke a specific thought sequence.

Memory

The reverse association s_a of s_i is called the *memory* of s_i.

Dissociation

There is actually nothing new about the concept of dissociation, which is defined as "the splitting off of certain mental processes from the main body of consciousness with various degrees of autonomy" (Hilgard, 1977, 1992). This definition, however, is too vague for our purposes. This definition seems to circumscribe at least three types of phenomena all of which could be termed "dissociation," but which are functionally different. The three types of dissociation are abstraction, autonomous multiprocessing and trance.

Dissociation is the mechanism by which processing becomes distributed to dominant and latent sequences. When both dominant and latent sequences are continuing at the same time, then there is parallel processing. The latent sequence becomes the trained automaton. Multiple parallel information processing, with or without awareness, seems to be at the basis of influencing cognition, affect and behavior.

What distinguishes the dominant from the latent sequences of dissociation is the disabling or enabling of certain cognitive functions from the latent sequence.

Abstraction as a type of dissociation

When the sequence of thoughts s_1, ..., s_i, ..., s_k, occurs often enough, the individual may remember that s_1 was the progenitor of s_k. Therefore, there may be the reverse association s_k to s_1 as well as the pattern association s_1 to s_k, such as a "linked list." When s_1 next occurs, the channel will be modified such that there is a greater probability that there will be a direct association s_1 to s_k as well as s_1 to the s_2 sequence. That is, the sequence s_2 ... s_{k-1} continues below the threshold of awareness, and awareness continues directly from s_1 to s_k. s_1 might represent the abstract symbol of the s_2 ... s_{k-1} sequence. *(See Figure 1)*

This dissociation (abstraction) function is a fundamental basis for learning. It seems that for reasons of energy

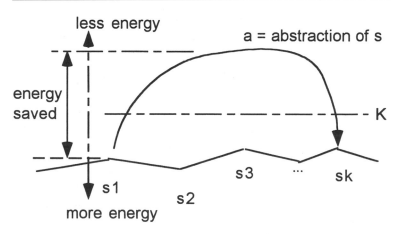

Figure 1: Association sequence, abstraction and relative energy.

conservation, latent sequences are more efficient than dominant sequences. That is longer sequences of thoughts may exist latently than can exist dominantly for the same expenditure of physiological energy. In existing latently some cognitive functions, such as critical thinking, are disabled.

The maximum rate at which the dissociation (abstraction) function may be implemented as well as the maximum length of latent sequences may be a basis for an accurate measure of thought processing efficiency or intelligence. Similar measures are applied to electronic parallel distributed computer systems. Abstraction in the mind is similar to a "linked list" in computer terminology insofar as one thought may be linked to multiple groups of thoughts. We have, through our experiences, abstracted from physiological functions to concepts. This abstraction process takes place as a very large number of small abstractions which take place during a lifetime. It is possible to access the underlying processes that form a given abstraction by self-reflection, memory or analysis.

Dissociation (autonomous multiprocessing) is a special function of cognition in which awareness is split into two portions, with the direct sequence, s_1 to s_k continuing as the dominant, conscious, aware sequence, and the s_2 to s_{k-1} sequence being subdominant, subconscious, or latent sequence. Simultaneously reading this book and scratching your arm is an example of this type of dissociation.

Trance Generating Loop

Thought sequences, thought associations, thought patterns, and abstract thoughts are quite important types of patterns, but there is another pattern which is even more important to the study of trance, and which I define as the "trance generating loop" or sometimes referred to as the TGL.

The dissociation which comes about from trance generating loops is at the basis of trance. This is nothing new. The hypnotist intones repeatedly that we are relaxed and happy. The shamans drum drones on in a monotonous beat. The alcoholic follows one drink by another. What perhaps is new is naming all of these repeated loops as causal to a specific type of dissociation that is uniquely characteristic of trance. The dissociation of trance is not abstraction and it is not a true autonomous multiprocessing.

Let us say that a thought, s_1, is followed by a known sequence of thoughts, s_2, ..., s_k, ..., s_n for which a subsequence eventually repeats, so that $s_k \rightarrow s_1$. This thought subsequence, $C = (s_1, \ldots s_k)$, of k elements I call a *trance generating loop (TGL)*. Thought sequences of this loop type include every type of thinking which starts and ends with the same thought. Hypnotic inductions are specific instances of trance generating loops, but trance generating loops include much more than traditional hypnotic inductions.

We can define some simple measures on a thought sequence $C = (s_1, \ldots, s_k)$ as follows: If C is a trance generating loop with k elements, k is simply the *elements* of C. The *repetitions* m of C is the number of times C is repeated.

Trance

When consciousness traverses c_1, there is a primary awareness e_1. When consciousness progresses to c_2, awareness is e_2, but there is also a residual awareness of e_1 which is denoted as e_1^2. At the end of the second repetition of c, m = 2, and at the same thought c_1 there exists the primary awareness e_1^1 and the secondary latent awareness e_1^2. At m =

3, we have at c_1, the new primary awareness e_1^{1} as well as the residual awareness e_1^{2} and e_1^{3}. If there is an attenuation of the awareness at the end of each repetition then $e_1^{1} > e_1^{2} > e_1^{3}$. At the same time, the total awareness at c_1 at the end of m repetitions must be the sum of all the partial awareness Σe_1^{m}. Each thought, c_i, in the trance generating loop has an associated awareness sum, Σe_i^{m}, which consists of the original part, c_i of the total awareness plus the residual awareness $\Sigma e_i^{m} - c_i$. This term represents the dissociated part of c_i and for all i in c the residual awareness is defined as the *dissociated trance plane* (DTP) of c, or, symbolically, $d = \Sigma e^{m} - c$. *(See Figure 2)*

The collective latent sum awareness, of c, denoted as d, when of sufficient collective energy will be subjectively experienced apart from the trance generating loop. It is this separate subjective experience we define as *trance*, a third

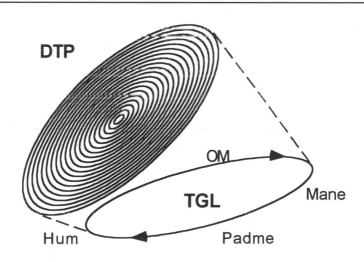

Figure 2: The Dissociated Trance Plane (DTP) which splits off from the TGL.

type of dissociation which is distinct from abstraction and from the automaton.

Dissociation as abstraction is an energy efficient cognition for processing patterns. Dissociation as automaton allows continuous patterns to be precessed autonomously without awareness. Dissociation as trance is an energy modification of awareness in order to process patterns in new ways.

Trance will occur under several conditions. It is helpful to discuss these conditions without regard to the specific content of the trance generating loop. The appearance of different types of trance or differing ASCs occurs because of a change in the underlying conditions of trance. This will become clear as the effect of varying conditions is discussed.

Limited Loop Length

When the number of elements of c is very large, there is a b such that $e_1(c_b) = 0$ for $n_t < b$ and $e_i(c_a) > 0$ for $a < n_t < b$. When $n > n_t$, c is indistinguishable from s since any looping of c will not contribute sufficient energy to bring about a dissociation.

Trance is most easily established by trance generating loops with $n < n_t$.

Sufficiency of Repetitions

When m, the number of times c is repeated, is too low then d is less than c and trance will not occur. As m becomes larger, d increases, until, at a certain point awareness may alternate between the planes of s and the dissociated trance plane.

Subjectively, a person becomes able to repeat c while at the same time entertaining slightly different other thoughts. These slightly different other thoughts appear to be "normal", but according to this model, they take place in the dissociated trance plane, and therefore are dissociated thoughts.

If m is sufficiently large before the "other thoughts" intervene, then sufficient energy can be generated to produce a stabile dissociated trance plane. However, if m is low or if "other thoughts" intervene, it is possible to produce multiple overlapping dissociated trance planes.

Light trances are produced when m is low. For example, music consists of many trance generating loops consisting of the multiple rhythms and melodies. As one listens to one specific rhythm or melody, when a certain value of m is reached, the melody is 'learned' and a dissociated trance plane is produced. When the dissociated trance plane is produced some cognitive functions are disabled and the 'conscious' mind is attracted to or picks another melody to listen to. The pattern repeats. The effect, mentally, is that the listener goes from one trance generating loop to the dissociated trance plane to another trance generating loop, etc. Both multiple — but countable — trance generating loops and dissociated trance planes exist. Although the trance generating loops are basically constant — they are part of the music — the dissociated trance planes come into existence and then disappear as the mind dissociates on each trance generating loop, the cognitive functions are disabled and the mind falls back into recognizing another aspect of rhythm or melody. It is these multiple dissociations — surfing on the dissociated trance planes, so to speak — that gives pleasure to the listener.

It should also be mentioned that as the mind is traversing one trance generating loop, it can certainly be attracted to another trance generating loop. *Attracted* means that there was an intervening dissociation as well as a disabling of a cognition. In these light trances, the dissociation, and the establishing of the dissociated trance plane, the disabling of a cognition and the termination of the trance may happen quite rapidly, within fractions of a second.

What the trance model provides is the structure of all trances — even at the millisecond level — as well as major decade-long trances. The trance model implies that there are many trances, some of which were not previously recognized as a type of trance.

Constancy of the trance generating loop

Trances which are already established may be modified by substituting elements in c. When elements are substituted c→ c', then the dissociated trance plane will also change.

So long as c remains constant, the dissociated trance plane appears to coincide with c and is indistinguishable from it. However, whenever there is a perturbation of c, or a substitution of any of the elements of c, that is c → c', then the dissociated trance plane will then subjectively appear distinct or separate from c'.

Trances may be interruptible by increasing the number of elements in the trance generating loop or by making substitutions to specific new elements of c which result in a decrease of the energy of the dissociated trance plane. This is not necessarily a straightforward operation; merely adding elements to the trance generating loop or making substitutions might only result in fantasies or hallucinations and behavior changes based on those hallucinations. Interrupting a trance means destroying the dissociated trance plane and reintegrating awareness in the s plane.

The existence of the dissociated trance plane depends first of all on the "loop" structure of c. Second, the persistence of the dissociated trance plane depends on some minimum value for m for an unperturbed c. Third, the manner of substitution, the rate of substitution and timing of c → c' may effect the persistence of the dissociated trance plane.

The dissociated trance plane also has a boundary in the sense that the disabling or modification of some cognitive functions limits or changes the area of consciousness in the dissociated trance plane. The shape of this boundary is quite important. In some cases the dissociated trance plane boundary excludes awareness of the body. In extraordinary cases the boundary may even include the awareness of personalities that have died. This boundary of the dissociated trance plane is very flexible and can change rapidly. It can also be modulated.

Persistence of Latency

For any specific thought c_i, as mentioned above, there is an associated awareness component e_i. This awareness component attenuates or becomes latent over a time interval (t_0, t_x). That is, for some large value of t_x, there is associated with each thought c_i an awareness function $a(c_i, t)$, such that $a(c_i, t_0) = e_i$ and $a(c_i, t_x) < \varepsilon$, an arbitrary small value.

A rapidly attenuating function will prevent trance from developing because an insufficient amount of energy would be available to create enough latent awareness to dissociate. Functions which attenuate relatively slow will result in trance. Hypnotics may promote a decrease in the attenuation rates of such awareness functions.

Speed of Loop

For trance generating loops of n components which are traversed in time t, there is an average speed of looping, v. When v is relatively high the effect of the attenuation functions becomes more important. Conversely, when v is relatively low, the effect on the created dissociated trance plane of the attenuation functions becomes less.

From a practical point of view, what this means is that whenever you do a task with few components relatively rapidly, you are more likely to develop a trance than if you were to do the same task slowly. To put it another way, an advertisement which is delivered at a slightly quicker pace would likely be more effective due to the result that more people would become dissociated. The same effect would be expected for hypnotic inductions.

In everyday life many people feel rushed, as though there was little time to do everything completely or satisfactory. As long as the tasks to be done don't repeat then trance is less likely. But if the tasks to be done are repetitive and rushed, trance is quite likely to develop. It is primarily for this reason that people who work with computers are likely to enter trance quite easily, especially when they are rushed and when the tasks to do are repetitive.

Nature of the dissociated trance plane

The dissociated trance plane requires less energy than the corresponding trance generating loop and therefore some cognitive functions are inhibited. The energy conservation profile of the dissociated trance plane enables abstraction and learning as well as multiprocessing to occur with greater efficiency than in the plane of s. It is due partly to the energy conservation nature of the dissociated trance plane that critical thinking, intellectual processes, judgments, accurate recall, decision-making are all inhibited. Awareness of the body may be reduced and analgesia may be present. Self-observation is enhanced. Hallucinations may be present.

What can be a source of confusion to researchers is the failure to recognize when dissociation starts. It would be difficult to assess dissociation by means of subjective reporting because with very strong dissociated trance planes many intellectual processes are inhibited, such as decision-making and other critical functions. Self-observation, itself, is a characteristic of dissociation. Therefore, in many cases the subject would not even realize when dissociation had occurred because the subject must be slightly dissociated in order to self-observe. It is for these reasons that precise subjective reporting of dissociation is unreliable. In cases of micro-dissociation such as when listening to music, it would be impossible to rely on subjective reporting. To show this, the reader is invited to listen to some music and to identify the trance generating loops as well as the dissociations. Make a check mark when the dissociation occurs and describe what your mind does as soon as it is dissociated. You can realize with this example how difficult relying on subjective reporting is for indicating dissociation.

Stability of the dissociated trance plane

The dissociated trance plane generally is not stabile. Normally, it is easily interrupted and it collapses. For example, if you see someone whose gaze is fixed, you can assume they are in a trance. If you say, "Hey, are you in a trance?" they snap out of it quite easily. Often a person will snap out of a trance because they start to think using disabled cognitive functions. As soon as some cognitive functions are required the dissociated trance plane will normally vanish.

The dissociated trance plane becomes stabile when there is a secondary order trance generating loop consisting of the dissociated trance plane and the original trance generating loop. (*See Figure 3.*)

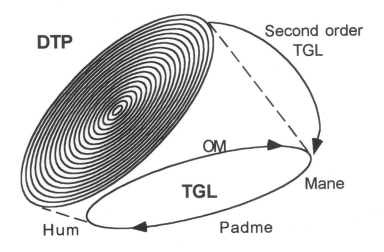

Figure 3: The second order TGL links the DTP with the TGL, forming a second order TGL. This second order TGL can also create a DTP.

Potentiated dissociated trance planes and constructive trance generating loops

When the dissociated plane changes from DTP → DTP' there is implied a change in the corresponding TGL→ TGL'. When TGL' does not exist, and comes into existence, the TGL' is called *constructive*. Likewise, when a portion or a section of a trance generating loop is enabled, a corresponding dissociated trance plane is potentiated.

The conditions under which dissociated trance planes are potentiated are called *triggers.*

A simple trigger word for a posthypnotic action may be a word which is a subset of a trance generating loop. The trance generating loop potentiates a dissociated trance plane as the association on this word and evokes an internal state. The

DTP may change to DTP' or construct a TGL' containing an action. Thus the sequence for a posthypnotic suggestion is t $\rightarrow$ TGL $\rightarrow$ DTP $\rightarrow$ DTP' $\rightarrow$ TGL' $\rightarrow$ action.

The Measure of Trance Force

Each of the elements of c_i has an associated awareness component e_i. The awareness component e_i is a vector of measurements one of which component measurements is the trance force, $W(e_i)$.

If the average value of the $W(e_i)$ is less than a value W_o, then trance will not develop. The reason is that the sum of the partial latencies d is partially dependent on W_o in such a way that a low W_o will not contribute the required latent effect in order to produce trance.

The energy, $W(e)$, required to sustain awareness e is a small but measurable biophysical quantity. The energy, $W(k)$, required to maintain d is also small, and, in general, when s = c, and n = 0, $W(k) < W(e)$. However, for a large n and for trance, d is greater than c. In this case, s is projected or reflected on the trance energy plane d and the projection, s', is maintained with a minimum of energy. The trance force appears to increase as the efficiency of maintaining a trance increases, that is, when a dissociated trance plane is maintained easily. In hypnosis, an easily maintained dissociated trance plane is often called a 'deep trance.' In a deep trance one would expect to measure a relatively strong W. It is a strong W which gives the sense of *weirdness* or *other-worldly* quality to deep trance. More than any other characteristic of trance, it is this *weird trance force,* which I will denote here as the WTF, which is remarkable as one defining characteristic of intense deep trance. (*See Figure 4*).

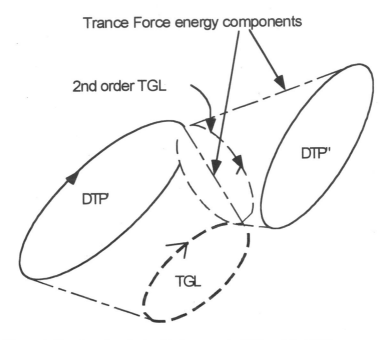

Figure 4: Showing the relationship between the TGL and the WTF

The trance force might not be a 'force' or 'energy' in the ordinary sense of physics. The trance force occurs only as a result of the existence of the dissociated trance plane. The more stabile the dissociated trance plane, the more intense the trance force.

The noticeable intensity of the trance force depends on several conditions. First the dissociated trance plane must be stable, because it is difficult to notice any trance force if there is no consistency. Second, the area of the dissociated trance plane must be large. This could mean that the dissociated trance plane was very sharp or elongated as when the mind is concentrated or the dissociated trance plane may be very large as when the mind has been trained by decades of meditation. Either way, a significant trance force will exist.

One way to create a strong trance force is to make a secondary or derived trance generating loop TGL → DTP → W, that is, to reward a strong trance force with an increase in the effectiveness of the trance generating loop. We call this a *secondary order trance generating loop*.

Secondary order trance generating loops are important in deep hypnotic traces, addictions and advanced yogic states.

The trance force, when it can be sustained as in a deep hypnotic trance, has important characteristics.

Since intense trance forces will involve large and stabile dissociated trance planes these dissociated trance planes will also be potent. That is, they will tend to construct derivative trance generating loops and potentiate dissociated trance planes. It is this potentiating effect of the trance force which gives the feeling of *weirdness* and which can cure warts, among its other so-called magical effects.

Agrippa said "the affection of the phantasy, when it vehemently intends itself, doth not only affect its own proper body, but also another's. So also the desire of witches to hurt, doth bewitch men most perniciously with steadfast looks ..." He also said, "philosophers advise that the society of evil, and mischievous men be shunned, for their soul being full of noxious rays, infects them that are near with a hurtful contagion ... the society of good, and fortunate men be endeavoured after, because by their nearness they do us much good."

The feeling of weirdness can also be felt during many kinds of occult activity. It may be common where there is a perception of spirits or ghosts. It is this feeling that makes your hair stand on end. It may be that the intense trance force is related to bio-energy or is derived from unknown chemical, electrical or magnetic system effects.

What may help to further describe the trance force and its effects is the following speculation. Normally, we live in the mahamaya which may be a very large trance force field. We are accustomed to living in this field, so it establishes our feeling of normalcy. When a person is in a very deep trance a locally intense trance force is created which may interfere with the local effect of the mahamaya. It is the interference which gives rise to the weirdness and to the sense of unreality.

When a deep trance is created for the purpose of making a wart disappear, the intense trance force created alters the local field in such a way that the wart cannot sustain itself. The exact mechanism is unknown but it may be related to projected bio-energy or derived from unknown chemical, electrical or magnetic system effects caused by the trance force or a modulation of this force.

Weirdness itself can be explained as a derived complex of biological, electrical, chemical and magnetic system changes experienced subjectively.

When a trance force can be sustained then it will be possible to determine how and in what way the trance force creates or interferes with local bio-energy, chemical, electrical or magnetic systems. Because in most normal situations the dissociated trance plane is not consciously sustainable, except in deep trance, the trance force will not often be created. When the trance force is created by deep trance it is often not under very good control, and therefore the exact effect of a specific trance force is difficult to determine. Not only that, but the lack of a good model for trance has made speculation as to the nature and characteristics of the trance force too uncertain until now.

Once good objective measures of trance have been established, including the existence, range and shapes of a dissociated trance plane as well as the trance force, it should be easier to find correlations between measurements on the trance force and objectively verifiable physical effects.

The first characteristic of the trance force is that it tends to bring into sympathy or alignment the other trance forces in other bodies or areas. This is the alchemical 'as above so below' magical phenomena. One can hypothesize that the trance force is a type of bio-magnetic energy which potentiates sympathetic phenomena. It is the operation of the trance force which causes warts to disappear by hypnotic suggestion, for example. It is the operation of the trance force which causes sympathetic magical phenomena to occur as a result of ritual magic or deep meditation. The trance force potentiates trance generating loops.

A second characteristic of the trance force is that it may be used in a sensate mode in which it is 'aligned' with other trance forces. The yogi or meditator who does this becomes aware of remote phenomena and the thoughts of others.

Specifically, for example, the large extended and quiescent trance force of a yogi may behave like a carrier over time and space as much as the mahayana is a carrier. Changes in remote bio-energy, electrical, chemical or magnetic systems may perturb or alter the quiescence of this carrier and transmit intelligence to the yogi who is aware of the meaning of such subtle changes in the trance force. Such changes would alter the yogis dissociated trance plane and construct knowledge as trance generating loops of hidden events. These trance generating loops would appear to such a yogi as recurring dreams, or ideas which persisted in coming into consciousness. These constructive trance generating loops also have this *looping* quality and that is one way they can be identified.

Therefore the trance force generally is both like an extensible sense and an extensible organ of action. Magicians, yogis, witches, shamans and others attempt to gain mastery over the trance force through meditation, ritual and sacrifice. To express the goals of magicians, yogis, etc. in my terms, they hope through various practices to find the magical formula or trance generating loop which will create the proper dissociated trance plane or altered state of consciousness and develop over time a stabile dissociated trance .plane and then to develop conscious control over and an increase of the trance force which will enable them to both be aware of subtle phenomena as well as to exercise a degree of control over the universe or at least their local portion of it.

Creating dissociated trance planes and trance forces over which a person can exercise some conscious control seems to be a matter of time and personal energy. It would be important not to waste time or energy on practices which are ineffective or which produce undesirable effects. The improper use or mismanagement of trance technology can easily produce all of the symptoms of pathological behavior including addictions and hallucinations. I would suggest, in fact, that we all wish to be masters of our universe, but, in fact, we have been seduced either through mismanagement of trance or outright trance abuse, into various types of pathological trances including a wide variety of trance addictions.

One of the problems in creating a trance is that the dissociated trance plane always causes a cognitive disabling. That is, as soon as you do something which gets you into trance, you 'lose' control. This, to many people, is like magic, and it can be frightening. McKenna describes a commonality of both schizophrenics and shamans in that "they may develop a fixed ideation on a narrow circle of significant ideas, omens, or objects often becoming so intense as to result in sleeploss or autohypnosis." The cognitive disabling that is produced along with vivid hallucinations may be responsible for the death and rebirth symbolism often found in shamanistic initiations and in the fully manifested shamanic trance.

Creating A Trance

To summarize the chronological steps of a trance creation:

1. Normal thinking; that is, thoughts, s, do not exhibit any repeating loops. In modern society, this is probably more rare than hoped for.

2. A trance generating loop starts for an induction period until the latent effect becomes stronger, that is, the dissociated trance plane is created and can exist apart from the trance generating loop.

3. A dissociation shift occurs at precisely the time when the strength of the dissociated trance plane exceeds that of the trance generating loop and becomes noticeable when the underlying c is perturbed to c'.

4. Awareness shifts to the dissociated trance plane. The trance starts. In this case, trance logic occurs in the dissociated part. Thought sequences which the person experiences are experienced in trance. Learning tends to be accelerated and thinking less critical. Hallucinations could be present, depending on the content of the original loop, c and prior triggers.

5. The trance generating loop stops or is interrupted. Depending on several factors, awareness may shift to s. When this occurs, we say that the trance has ended and that one is "awake." The trance is terminated, and awareness shifts from the dissociated trance plane to s. The dissociated trance plane disappears. Trance logic stops. There remains a potentiated

trance, a trace of the dissociated trance plane which is abstracted and unconscious. This potentiated trance is the potentiated dissociated trance plane and any c' sequences.

6. Post trance effects — that is, constructive trance generating loops — may occur whenever the potentiated dissociated trance plane is triggered by an appropriate s.

Identifying the trance generating loop

Identifying a trance is foremost an effort in identifying the one or more trance generating loops that induce the trance. The first difficulty is to realize that the trance generating loop may not have any content at all similar to what the trance appears to be about. The trance generating loop, after all, merely induces the dissociative experience. The second difficulty in identifying the trance generating loop is that often there are no human terms available to accurately describe the "thought objects" which constitute the content of the trance generating loops. A third difficulty is that the dissociated trance plane implies a partially disabled cognition and awareness. A fourth difficulty is that trance generating loops may be of extremely short duration. I believe that these difficulties are at the root of a failure to understand what trance is all about.

The exact content of the trance generating loop is often not so obvious. For example, reading a book or watching television in which a long story is told "seems" to be the primary trance generating loop with a large number of elements. The book or the video tape which seems to be responsible for producing the trance can be played or experienced over and over. It would seem that therefore the book or the video tape itself was the primary trance generating loop. It is not. It is the secondary order trance generating loop. The sequence of input in the case of a book or television images is not a closed loop, but only a linear sequence, s. If this were the only cognitive sequence then by definition of the model, trance would not occur.

It is known by measured changes in alpha states that an ASC occurs within 30 seconds or so of the commencement of watching television. The primary trance generating loop in this case is not the elements in the long story sequence, s, but is the loop between the image on the screen and the physiological reactions of the viewer which produces the desire to continue the experience. That is, the viewer looks at the images on the screen, associates to his own experiences, and this association access creates a desire to resolve or repeat the actual experience. The viewer therefore continues to look at the screen in order to obtain fulfillment of this desire. This trance generating loop is quite short and is the most important loop which induces the trance associated with television viewing. Broadcasting noise or images which do not create the associations or which do not create a desire to resolve or repeat an accessed association will not create the desire to continue to look at the screen. In such a case there would be no trance generating loop and therefore no trance. Those people who are already in an addictive trance could, of course, be fascinated by simple video noise.

The Experience of Trance

The collective latent sum awareness d is experienced in some sense as real during trance in spite of the fact that d is derived from an external source. In the case of television, the trance generating loop creates the trance effect and the continuous television images, s, are subjectively experienced while in this trance, that is, the awareness of the viewer is from the dissociated plane and not the generating loop. The effect of the trance helps to create the illusion that the images are "other," that is, that the television images have an independent reality.

If the viewing of the television images were not done from the dissociated trance plane, viewing television would be exhausting and unrewarding. However, viewing television while in trance is relaxing and enjoyable because energy consuming critical functions are disabled. That is to say, when you watch television, trance logic is operant.

Trance Logic

Trance logic is defined by Orne (1959) as an ability to mix physical perceptions with hallucinations and Bowers (1983) contends that trance logic is a form of dissociation, which leads me to conclude that trance logic operates in d but not in s.

If trance can be created using a trance generating loop then the content of the trance generating loop can be "learned" as soon as dissociation occurs. That is, the energy requirements to maintain the trance generating loop becomes substantially less as soon dissociation occurs. Less energy requirements implies that some cognitive functions are disabled and that some other cognitive functions may be enhanced. The change in the energy requirements occurs in any trance, but is more obvious in deep trance.

The implications of a change in energy requirements are as follows:

1. Critical judgement is decreased or disabled
2. There is a change in body awareness sensations
3. There is an increase in literalism and primary process thinking (images and symbols more than words) increases.

4. Hypermnesia or perceived enhanced recall of memories; or amnesia, selective forgetting.
5. Disabling or limiting of volition
6. Inaccurate sense of reality
7. Vivification or Hallucinations
8. Fixed attention
9. Involvement in inner processes or contact with the unconscious mind.
   10. Other cognitive changes

When any of the above characteristics of trance logic are present, the existence of a trance is presumable. To determine more characteristics of the trance, it is necessary to discover the trance generating loop of the trance. When trance generating loops involve triggers, it is important to determine the trance generating loops of the underlying trances.

Ordinary Trances

Trance can be produced by the repetition of mantras, by chanting, by exposure to any repeated images. Regular drumbeats will produce trance. Formal hypnotic inductions will produce trance. Pacing or mirroring or imitating the gestures, body movements or affect of one person by another will produce trance. Complex human and ordinary activity such as falling in love, being absorbed in a TV program, marching in a parade, and even commuting to work all involve trance. Trance, when it does occur, occurs because the energy requirements of the dissociated trance plane are less than the energy requirements of the primary trance generating loop. Many ordinary activities would be impossible if it were not for the energy conservation effects of trance.

Why is energy conservation important? I believe that energy conservation in the trance generating loop allows energy usage in the dissociated trance plane. This energy usage allows the boundary of the dissociated trance plane to change. What psychologists have noted as characteristics of trance logic are only partly the result of this change in the topology and energy usage of the dissociated trance plane. The trance force comes into existence partly as a result of increased stability of the modified dissociated trance plane.

Spontaneous Trance

Occasionally a person will seem to slip into a trance without a discernible reason. Daydreaming is an example of this. There are many potentiated dissociated trance planes which can be triggered by sequences or subsequences of the trance generating loops which produced a specific dissociated trance plane. Partly dissociated trance planes are related to learning and partly to the autonomous nervous system, therefore it is possible to cause a fully developed trance by invoking prior trance states through subsequences of the trance generating loops. Professional hypnotists are fully aware of this fact. To analyze why a spontaneous trance develops, it is only necessary to look for triggers on trance generating loops.

Spiritual Trance

In the case of c = the mantra, *Om Mane Padme Hum*, the elements of c is four, and, if you repeat this mantra 108 times, this trance generating loop would have loops of 108. A Tibetan Lama may say, "One repetition may not be enough to achieve enlightenment, but 100,000 repetitions of 108 may be enough." In this case, the loops of c must be 10,800,000 to possibly achieve enlightenment, or certainly an ASC.

If the strength of the trance or the duration of the effect of the trance depends partly on the number of repetitions and not on the content of the trance generating loop, then there are two possible reasons for the existence of trances with spiritual content. The first reason is that dissociation produces a high potential for hallucination. The second reason is that motivating a spiritual seeker to generate trance generating loops with high repetition counts may be more possible when the content is related to the effect one wishes to produce. If you want to "see" God, then it will be easier to use a name of God only because you will be more motivated to generate trance generating loops with higher repetition counts than if you were to repeat "light bulb" or "banana skin". However, the model implies that very high repetition counts of "banana skin" will also enable a devotee to "see" God or at least Godlike banana skins.

I do not wish to be specifically provocative but the somewhat mechanical nature of trance seems to work regardless whether the content of the trance generating loop relates to Allah, Buddha, Christ, Hitler, Elvis Presley, the Earth Spirit or Zoraster.

The content of the trance generating loop does not affect the primary production of the dissociated trance plane; however, once the trance starts then the content of the trance generating loop will have hypnotic effects when specific elements of the trance generating loop triggers other dissociated trance planes or when the primary trance generating loop is modified.

With certain other conditions already mentioned large dissociated trance planes will have associated strong or intense trance forces which potentiate other trance generating loops. These constructive trance generating loops will indeed be magical, but again have nothing to do with the content of the primary trance generating loops. Falsely associating a specific trance generating loop with an intense and 'magical' trance force is simply ignorance of how trance really works.

Pathological Trance

When a dissociated trance plane is produced which is so strong that some cognitive functions are disabled over long periods of time, inappropriate behaviors, hallucinations, limited options and many other characteristics of pathology will be seen. When a trance cannot be terminated due to multiple secondary order trance generating loops, in my opinion the condition is pathological.

God and Mummy loves me, and its variations may be a trance generating loop for some people. While the number of elements is five, this trance generating loop in some cases may have been mentally and emotionally repeated *more* than 10,800,000 times. In such cases of large n of the primary trance generating loop, I would suspect that a very strong dissociated trance plane could be produced along with concomitant potential hallucinations both negative and positive of all kinds. It seems to me that the operant mechanism for ASCs as well as trance based pathologies is the basic trance generating loop structure and the persistence and strength of the resulting dissociated trance planes. The latency of the underlying abstractions are responsible for the content of the ASC.

As a final example of how a trance generating loop may start in traumatic situations: a man rapes a woman. The woman repeats some sequence c "this is not happening to me" mentally or emotionally to escape her fear and the pain. The trance generating loop creates a dissociated state. The dissociated trance plane creates the subjective experience that "it is not happening to me," and the woman experiences the rape while in a trance state. The physical experience however is still happening, and these experiences perturb the trance state, that is, c → c' and secondary and tertiary trance generating loops and dissociated trance planes are created. The trance state operates with trance logic, that is, learning is accelerated and uncritical. When the rape is over and the trance is terminated, the associated abstracted patterns, the "anchors" and "triggers", remain potential to recreate both the dissociated states as well as the physical experiences. Presumably therapeutic intervention depotentiates the triggers and dissociated trance planes. From the point of view of trance theory, therapeutic intervention for rape victims must start before secondary order trance generating loops are established.

If subsequent experiments prove that this systems approach is patent, then extensions to the model to more accurately describe specific social, psychological, pathological conditions and therapeutic strategies would be a next step.

Pathological Trance and Addiction

Normal Trances

I make an assumption about what is desirable in life, and I should state it explicitly. I assume that a robust life is a life of variety and wide options, and that an impoverished life is a life with few options and little variety. Life naturally contains limits and limits help to restrain chaos and thus to free a certain kind of energy. Although there are many people of the opinion that all limits are bad, I feel that limits alone are not bad, in fact, limits are necessary to empower creativity. However, certain types of strict limits in life seem to imply the presence of a pathological state or at least delusions about lack of personal power. There is a delicate balance between the limits which empower personal growth and the limits which crush human spirit.

One way to find this balance is to realize that within any personal psychological reality there is a set of changing stimuli and response potentials. A behavior is a pair of specific stimulus with its response and a behavior results in a new stimulus which joins other stimuli in creating the personal psychological reality. Theoretically, the responses that may exist for a given set of stimuli can be counted. The number of such potential responses is often thought of as the "richness" of a person's life. A relatively low number of potential responses or options indicates a relatively impoverished reality.

A healthy, normal psychological life seems to be one in which there is a rich set of stimuli and a rich set of responses. Furthermore, the pattern of behavior tends not to be rigidly repetitive and this rich variety seems to allow both personal growth and to stimulate others in their own search for variety and richness in life. On the other hand, an addictive personality could be characterized as one in which there are few responses and the pattern of behavior is generally repetitive.

What I find to be interesting is to apply the principles of trance theory to a wide variety of individual and institutional behaviors that appear to be rigid or repetitive — that is, presumable trances — and try to determine what the trance generating loops are and what the characteristics of the dissociated trance planes are and how one might describe any created trance forces.

A person has the potential to be in a normal trance as soon as their attention is limited. Ordinary concentration, when the mind is focused on a specific problem or thought, sets one of the conditions for a normal trance to occur. Intense pleasure, when the mind is engaged in joyful or exciting repetitive activity, sets a condition for trance and may, for many people, become a trance. When one is daydreaming, with no specific direction of the thoughts, with a certain repetition of thoughts, one is in a normal trance. The general characteristic of these normal trance states seems to be that thoughts repeat and there is a limiting of attention; however, they can be easily interrupted. What makes a normal trance *normal* is primarily that it is easily interrupted. That is, specifically, disturbing the trance generating loop makes the dissociated trance plane collapse. Depending on many factors, such as the presence of secondary trance generating loops, or if the dissociated trance plane is stabile enough so that disturbing the trance generating loop only makes more or different dissociated trance planes — hallucinations — such trances would appear less normal and more weird. Certain of them we can term *pathological* and we can describe them in terms of trance theory.

Sharing Normal Trance

We share trances for the effects of trance; that is, for the effects brought about by an altered cognition space.

With less awareness of pain whether it is emotional, physical or ontological, and with less awareness of the wide variety of choices that exist in an enabled reality, the person in trance happily chooses among an impoverished and smaller set of options.

Life, perhaps, would be too difficult if people were always aware of their bodies, always had a perfect memory and always made perfect judgements and were always aware of the infinite possibilities of life. Because most people cannot stand pain, because most people fear chaos, uncertainty and death, most people enter into social, institutional and mutual personal trances in order to *reduce* awareness. Perhaps, in the not too distant past, life was uncertain — in times of war, or in hunger, poverty, fear and abuse situations — and it made sense to hide and to create trance by singing ourselves songs, or saying prayers, or by putting our minds on certain constant images or visions. This is indeed how natural trances are created; and the usual reason is to hide from something.

By a mutual trance, I mean that each of us in various ways and by social behavior supports an impoverished awareness in others. Our purposes in supporting impoverished awareness are: to be able to have some peace ourselves, to reduce the noise and the pain. Again, the reason for this is to reduce our awareness of the reality of chaos and escape the pain of the human condition. There is also some pleasure in entering trance in spite of the fact that trance reduces awareness.

If we speak of degrees of trance, it is my opinion that there is only a difference in degree between passively watching TV, ordinary rational thought and rigorous scientific thought, religious fervor, addictive states, and the states of mind belonging to mass murderers. All of the mind states above represent differing degrees of trance states.

There is also a strong similarity between addictions, hypnotic trance and "altered states of consciousness." All of these "non-normal" states come about first by the progressive narrowing of perception and the limiting of awareness to a single, or at most very few objects of attention. The narrowing of attention can be induced by drugs, chanting, television, etc. Second, an association must be made which connects every attempt to make the attention wider to an effort to make the attention more narrow. This association will serve to concentrate attention on the objects of attention. Third, when the association is strong enough, the original impulse to narrow attention can be removed. The reason is that the strong association already created will continue the attention toward the few objects.

Tribes, cults, societies and nations inculcate restricted social behaviors through trance, training, customs and laws because it requires simply too much cognitive processing to understand the unusual. In the abysmal past, the unusual were simply killed. Nowadays trance helps to limit awareness and therefore the more unusual have more of a chance to exist. This in itself is probably a positive evolutionary phenomenon.

It may seem bizarre to advocate the development of more intense trances and limited awareness and more impoverished realities as a global solution to social ills, yet, with drug addiction, religions and television isn't that precisely what seems to be happening? Let's understand what it is we are really doing and do it more efficiently! In America, where more than 95% of the homes have television and the daily average time spent in front of a television is in excess of five hours, people may believe themselves to be informed, but their realities are impoverished.

When people walk around with their virtual reality helmets, trance music reverberating in the vacuum of inner space, they may believe themselves to be 'connected' to the Host and King of the information mountain, but they will be only aware of a certain limited class of toxic atmospheric discharges, and social inequities. They will be unaware of their own abuse.

In lieu of a fearless awareness of an enriched life, most people have chosen the way of trance. Let it be. Tranceless awareness is not for everyone.

Habits

A habit usually is a long and complex trance generating loop and therefore when done only a few times represents a weak trance, that is, a trance with an unstable dissociated trance plane. Yet, when the habit is done hundreds or thousands of times, the behavior may become compulsive and appear like an addiction. In such a case, there is a more stabile trance force with constructive trance generating loops.

Socially or economically reinforced habits such as shaking hands, smoking cigarettes, having sex in the missionary position, wearing clothes when in society, answering the telephone when it rings, flushing the toilet after it is used, coming home after work and turning the TV on, all represent habits that are socially or economically supported in most countries of this world. Often the individual effort needed to break such trances is more than is possible to do. Such social habits or trances represent deep trances with trance force components and secondary order constructive trance generating loops.

To break such trances increases the awareness of individual chaos, uncertainty, and pain. The sense of chaos, or fear, uncertainty and pain is the reaction that is caused by attempting to change or modify the trance force.

One could characterize this situation as an entrancement by magic.

One must be quite courageous to attempt to modify a trance force. In addition, the trance analysis needed to break a trance is often a complicated and difficult undertaking. There is also no guarantee that even if the underlying trance generating loops were known it would be possible to break the trance easily.

Love Trances

Love is a human emotion which is created socially often through a period of courtship and intimacy, desire and fantasy, physical contact and orgasm.

The courtship, when it exists, often or typically occurs during primary trance inductive social situation such as dancing, listening to music, etc. These primary inductive social trance situations may produce many of the disabled cognitive conditions characteristic of trance, including faulty or failed memory, hallucinations, fixed attention, lack of volition, inability to make judgements, increased self-observation, dissociation, etc.

Love also has secondary inductive characteristics, insofar as courting individuals often speak of family, feelings, etc. These subjects often contain triggers to prior trance states. For example, when two people speak of personal experiences within their own family experiences, they may use words which trigger prior trance states. Courting and petting also may trigger somatic trances. Heavy petting will trigger prior somatic trance states including dissociation, lack of volition, fixed attention, etc.

When petting is coupled with physical release or relaxation such as orgasm, there is established a secondary order trance generating loop to enable these trance states.

The trance generating loop of love is characteristic of an addictive or hypnotic trance in the sense that the pathway of the secondary trance generating loop contains some external or physical component, and the dissociated trance plane leads back to the physical component.

There are many types of love trances. Some love trances may also have high components of the trance force but usually there are secondary order trance generating loops present.

The Social Effects of Narrowed Perceptions

Wise people have known that things don't last, that "all is vanity." The pain and disappointments of life tend to teach a receptive mind that "all that glitters is not gold." Maybe it is simply radioactive and it is killing you.

In order to make wise decisions, it is necessary to have a wider state of awareness and consciousness, and not a narrow one. It is necessary to have an overview of the long-range consequences of our decisions and not the narrow ones which come from the immediate satisfaction of personal desire. With so many desirable objects in the world, and so much new information, how do we increase our awareness and wisdom?

Many kinds of consciousness raising activities try to promote the possibility that there are other ways to see or to understand life. In a larger field of awareness of possibilities, a more mature and integrated awareness can develop, resulting in less fear of chaos as well as a more open potential of being.

Psychologists and psychiatrists try to widen the perceptions of their clients, to promote new ways of handling stress and uncomfortable feelings without escape or denial. It is these wider perceptions, with more robust psychological options of action in life which enriches life, and not necessarily more material possessions in life.

Psychically, the narrowing of perception and the limiting of options or making an object of the sources of personal happiness, personal salvation and personal betterment gives rise to ideas such as heaven, God, a Saviour, a cult of personality, brand loyalty and patriotism. Generally, the narrowing of perception produces hypnotic trance. In severe or pathological cases, the narrowing of perception produces paranoia, schizophrenia, violence, and addictions of all sorts.

Making an object out of our perceived source of happiness, salvation and betterment also promotes the idea that there are "good", "moral", or "ethical" things and behaviors. That is, there is the perception that some 'things' are better than other 'things'. And therefore some things are worse, or even "sinful." It is often believed by some people that dope is bad, guns are bad and money is "the root of all evil". These beliefs about dope, guns and money come naturally from the idea that "things could be better, and the world would be a whole lot better if (dope, guns, or money) didn't exist." There is really no justification for empowering an object or a thing with the qualities of good or evil, except in the case of a narrowed perception and hallucinated projections. But it is precisely this narrowed perception or the hallucinated projections from the dissociated trance plane on to the object which causes dysfunction to arise in the psyche, in the individual, and in all social institutions and in the environment itself.

Learning something new utilizes dissociation as abstraction, but employing the hallucinated projections from the dissociated trance plane is not learning.

Sometimes it is argued that calling a thing "good" is merely a shorthand way of saying something more complex and a short-hand way of providing a sort of synopsis, saving time and avoiding a detailed description. The "good/bad" judgement is merely a way that an experienced authority can communicate the bottom line to someone, without needing to go through a tedious list of conditions, and assumptions that underlie the ultimate judgement. Of course, the experienced authority can have false experience, or have a hidden agenda which makes any judgements coming from such an authority immediately suspicious. Furthermore, the conditions may be falsely enumerated, and the logic supporting the "good" judgement may also be faulty. Usually, people find themselves arguing the "goodness" of a thing on precisely these terms: that one or the other has faulty assumptions or faulty logic, or has a hidden agenda which biases perception. Someone may ultimately admit that they only have a "belief" that the thing is "good," or that their judgement is merely a personal opinion which cannot be supported by the facts. When there are multiple hallucinated projections on to objects, people and situations, one belief will compete with all other beliefs, arguments will abound between one group with the Holy Writ against another group that is divinely inspired. It is quite simply lunatics arguing among delusions.

The self-searching individuals naturally wish to escape this madness. Some will evolve to new forms. Many will escape by dropping out. Dropping out often takes an addictive form. Alcohol, drugs, religion, work, overconsumption, and TV are only a few of the more obvious forms of addictions. In many cases the dropping out takes the form of a desire to be in a trance which is induced or supported by substances like alcohol and drugs, or by social forms such as religion, work, consumption, or by more individual forms such as TV, love, overeating, violence etc.

Economic Effects

When the individual suffers, the family suffers. Dysfunctional, dropped-out, individuals in addictive trances place tremendous pressures on their families. As individuals experiencing the results of family members going through addictive behaviors are themselves stressed, it is no wonder that families disintegrate. When families don't disintegrate, there is often the side effects of child and spouse abuse or more serious social crimes. Disintegrated families result in homeless or nomadic gangs. Nomadic gangs are common in cities and are symptomatic of the underlying dysfunction. Cities become more difficult to manage when family and individual dysfunction become widespread and affects social institutions. After all, the social institutions can only reflect the individuals that run them.

Former Governor Lamb of Colorado has identified the *dysfunctional institution* in his own state and recognizes the same institutional dysfunctions on all levels of government. Widespread individual and institutional dysfunction destroys social assets. Dysfunction destroys people, jobs, the connectivity of the social fabric and the pertinence of institutions. Institutions cease to be efficient and themselves become dysfunctional. While social resources and government assets can support dysfunctional institutions in times of chaos, in extreme cases and over the long term, these resources and assets eventually are depleted, worn out, used up and become useless or self-destructive. This characteristic of extremely dysfunctional institutions is more common in third-world countries.

Social dysfunctions can all be traced back to the pernicious effects of hypnotic and addictive trance at the individual level.

Pathological Trances

Addiction can be better understood if we think of it not merely as "substance abuse," or performance addiction, but as a form of an impoverished reality that is maintained by a trance. Limited awareness, tunnel vision, the special characteristic that identifies a dysfunctional, impoverished reality, also identifies a type of trance state that may be also a characteristic of all addictions.

While pathological trances are not at all desirable, most people nearly all of the time are either in a pathological trance or are engaged in trying to get others into trance. It is precisely pathological trance, not the yogic trance, that permeates most of our waking social reality. It seems to me that once we can identify these pathological trances on a personal and social level we can take steps to avoid them.

Perhaps the most important aspect of pathological trance is that it creates an unawareness or a "sleeping state". When your thoughts are limited in variety and your attention becomes fixed, the fixation alters perceptions, can create dream states, visions and hallucinations. In this sleeping state you are unaware of new information. Entranced by the street magician, you are unaware that the pickpocket has removed your wallet. The pathological trance state can create illusions which do not exist and cause the failure to perceive what does exist. Not all trances are pathological; the trance state of a yogi can be a tool to illuminate what is not normally perceived.

Addiction

It is estimated that over 95% of the American population have one or more "addictions." Such addictions include drug and alcohol addictions (now termed "substance abuse" to include cocaine, psychedelics, caffeine, nicotine, as well as alcohol, sugar, chocolate and junk-food), TV addiction, work-related addictions, sex and love addictions, food related addictions, computer addictions and other behavioral or performance addictions. Addictions commonly share the characteristic that a socially dysfunctional behavior is present and the addict has progressively fewer and fewer performance options resulting in an impoverished reality. High percentages of addiction are found not only in America. The ex-Soviet Union has its problems with vodka. India and the Middle East have their opium addicts and Switzerland and Japan have their work junkies. The personal life disruption and social costs are well-documented and the costs are probably well underestimated.

Alcohol addiction is a worldwide phenomenon. Even strict Islamic and Hindu cultures have their share of alcoholics. Alcohol is widely available in all industrial nations and cultures, including the ex-Soviet Union and Japan. Alcohol addiction is merely one way that addiction manifests, yet the social costs of alcohol addiction alone are immense.

Drug addiction too is a worldwide phenomenon. The drugs may change depending on the culture, the law and the severity of punishment. In the case of tobacco, it has been shown that nicotine is more addictive than heroin, yet in many parts of the world the consumption of nicotine is not only tolerated, but actually encouraged. The long-term health effects of tobacco use, while widely known, are ignored. The use of drugs, whether nicotine, caffeine, heroin, cocaine, marijuana, designer drugs or sugar has, like alcohol, long-term, immense social costs.

Drug Switching

The fact that addictions can be substituted somewhat easily may give a clue as to a therapeutic approach to addictions in general. Bandler and Grinder have shown that a process of pacing and leading can, over time, limit awareness and induce trance. With appropriate conditions, it may be possible to pace and lead addictive personalities into a wider and richer reality. In this sense, addicts can be "deprogrammed," without programming them into another addiction. The general goal is to program them in a rich type of reality where the subject of a past addiction exists, but along with a much more numerous set of attractive possibilities. When this occurs, it would be quite impossible to distinguish a prior addict from a "normal" person by behavior alone. It is certainly not desirable to negatively reinforce addictive syndromes. To do so runs the risk of modeling "drug switching" which is not a true cure.

It is known that one addiction can be substituted for another. For example, alcoholics can be induced to trade their alcohol addictions for a type of quasi-religious addiction (Alcoholics Anonymous). Alcoholics Anonymous (AA) programs are also "successful" with sex and love addicts, overeaters, Synanon, etc. Some heroin addicts can be induced to swap their heroin for methadone treatment. Therapists know that addictions are often found together, such as cigarettes and alcohol, and that the personality which is addicted to one substance or practice can be induced to either add other addictions or to swap them for others.

It is often thought that addictions come about through the stress of modern life, through childhood experiences, through trauma and disability, or that they may be genetically influenced. No one seems to know for certain, perhaps because addictions are so prevalent it is not possible to know what a nonaddictive state is like.

A great deal of inconsistent social, religious, personal, economic and political energy is spent in attempting to rid the world of the substance of an addiction. Except for societies which employ ruthless and absolute methods, the energy spent in riding the world of the "sinful substances" does not seem either very successful nor cost-effective. There are arguments that the anti-sinful substance zealots may themselves be dysfunctional in addictive and pathological ways.

Religious Addictions

Religious addictions seem harmless enough. A 1990 study of 113,000 people around the United States by the Graduate School of the City University of New York found that 90% of Americans identify themselves as religious. Born-again Christians, scientologists, Islamic fundamentalists, Jehovah's Witnesses, Masons, Baptists, Buddhists, Hindus, Methodists, Lutherans, Catholics, Jews, and Mormons usually have no other bad habits than occasionally beating on a book or selling something. Since the religious have fewer other "bad" habits, and seem to promote a certain tribal social adhesion, religions are not usually thought of as being symptomatic of problems, but rather, perhaps, as part of the solution. On the other hand, religious addiction often carries with it an intransigence and intolerance of different points of view that can be as dangerous as a drug addict with a loaded gun. When religious fervor is combined with the rule of law and armed with deadly force, religious addicts effectively prevent the evolution of a better type of human being.

Religious cults often use methods that will induce trance. Peer pressure, confessional types of testimonials, sense deprivation, lack of contradicting testimony, hysteria, hyper-emotionalism all contribute to constrain awareness and to increase suggestibility. Repetition continued over time will give rise to trance states, which with second order trance loops can certainly become addictive. Confession, for example, used as a catharsis, is a second order stress-relieving trance loop which reinforces the belief trance state.

Addiction can be better understood if we think of it not merely as "substance abuse," or performance addiction, but as a form of hypnotic trance that is maintained by a second order trance loop. Limited awareness, tunnel vision, the special characteristic that identifies a dysfunctional, impoverished reality, also identifies these types of pathological trance states that may be also a characteristic of all addictions.

Meditative trance states, related to hypnotic trance states, can also be termed as addictive if they are an end in themselves. Religious fervor, as a state which feeds upon itself without end, is also quite definitely an addiction in the definition of the model. Certain political and power syndromes also may be termed addictive if they have the characteristic that results in an impoverished reality.

The trance aspect of addiction deserves some comment.

In extreme addictions there may be no other awareness except the desire for the addictive substance and how to get it. Presumably, it is because of the limited awareness on a "substance" that got such substances such a bad name. It is not easy or convenient to blame a pattern or a process, since patterns and processes are so hard to identify, and don't occupy either space have weight or can be taxed.

Addiction to Television

The trance-induction potential of television is well-known and is used commercially for manipulating consumer tastes as well as other ideas. However useful television is for commercial and control reasons, it cannot be reasonably argued that promoting an impoverished reality is, in the end, really socially beneficial. Or can it?

The addiction to TV, for example, comes about first by having a mild interest in a specific TV program, and the narrowing of perception to the TV screen and listening to the voices and music, watching the scenes as they develop. Second, pleasurable associations through the use of triggers within the program should stimulate fantasies, hallucinations and dreams as a means of escape from everyday responsibilities or stress. In general, if a viewer likes a specific program, this association is easily made. TV producers spend a lot of effort to make TV productions pleasurable and escapist. Third, when there is no more stress and no more everyday responsibilities the pleasure that can be derived from watching TV must be high enough so that it is immaterial whether the use of TV is specific to stress removal or not. The addiction to TV will then be established.

Work Addictions

The person who can put long, continuous hours at a difficult job may only be capable to doing this if in a trance. The pleasures of an engaging job can produce feelings of timeless states. Repetitive jobs narrow the attention to only the work at hand. Part of the mind is engaged in the job, but another part of the mind is free to dream. The dream-state produced is exactly characteristic of trance. In this dream-state, the work is being performed, but the worker is not necessarily aware of working. He may be visualizing a beach, having sexual or power fantasies or other hypnoidal and hypnotic dreams. The worker seems aware, but is really in a trance with reduced awareness.

Work addicts are almost revered for their devotion to the duty to work. Calvin and Zwingli have convinced entire societies that the person who works and makes money is closer to God and has most assuredly has an eternal lease in one of heaven's plushier communities. Employers love work addicts because this devotion enhances profit. Work addictions are not limited to any one particular industry. As a professional computer consultant, I have seen how some employers shamelessly exploit willing computer programmers who are addicted to computers.

Trance in the work place makes it easier to control information and employees. If an employee only does the job in front of his nose and knows neither what others are doing nor how they do it, that employee will never become a threat to the owners of the business nor raise embarrassing social or political questions. One presumes — falsely — that the owners of a business would be the only ones who would be aware of what their business is really doing. Yet, owners are themselves in trance and many times keep their attentions only on the "bottom line." They, too, may not be aware of the social or environmental impacts of their business. Unfortunately, one of the disastrous side-effects of most trances is that they not only inhibit awareness but also they disable communication. One cannot communicate what one is not aware of.

Work related addictions first require that the perception is narrowed to the work or to work-related things and activities. Second, non-work related activity should be perceived as a source of stress, i.e. something to be avoided. The rewards of work should be limited to the perfection of the work itself, so that work is the means to the end. Finally, when the work-pleasure or the perfection-pleasure can sustain itself, the reason for work can be progressively reduced or removed. The stress produced will serve to drive the worker harder into his work, rather than reduce his production or concentration on work.

Organizational Effects of Trance

The most serious social side effect of pathological work trances is the resulting reduced awareness and disabled communication. Communication of information is critical for any system to function. Human systems as well as computer systems, ecological, biological, political and social systems and more all require clear, accurate, timely communication of information in order to function properly. The lack of clear, accurate, or timely communication between individuals is the basis for misunderstandings, disappointments, hurt feelings, resentment, and violence. The human, economic, agricultural, industrial and social systems that rely on people who are in pathological trance will have and do have disastrous breakdowns.

Pathological trance is unfortunately almost universally encouraged within business, military and governmental organizations. The more an employee can with single-minded determination execute the orders and policies of his organization, the more that employee is rewarded, promoted and respected. Single-mindedness, however, is indicative of trance and possibly a pathological trance. And the existence of a trance always implies that there are areas where the employee is unaware. Therefore, the single-mindedness that is rewarded in many large institutions actually contributes to long-term organizational dysfunction.

When organizations inadvertently encourage trance in their employees, and since trance disables communication, then there can be no surprise why there are system dysfunctions in business, the military and in government.

When, unlike a yogi, we do not choose our trances, and we are unaware of the types and nature of the pathological trances in our lives, then there are things we are unaware of. What we are unaware of causes more human suffering than the sometimes painful knowledge of the truth. One goal of a robust life is to be as aware as possible of our real options. When our unconscious pathological trances cripple our options the result is often disaster and tragedy in our personal lives, our society and in the environment.

Related to work addiction is a phenomenon more akin to what people often appreciate as "artistic inspiration" or artistic drive. An artist may spend long hours with a project which consumes his energy, perhaps stresses his family and finally results in a creation. What distinguishes this artistic drive from addiction is that the artistic drive is not a closed loop. That is, eventually the behavior comes to an end. However, if the behavior had no end, but repeated with an eventual decrease in response options, therapists would term the behavior dysfunctional and perhaps even "addictive." If the behavior had no end other than a "life style," for example, a therapist could readily identify the behavior as an addiction of a sort which does not end.

If the goal of therapists is trance termination and enrichment of reality, it is also interesting to consider the type of society that might become when we all wake up.

If you really want to get into a pathological trance and stay there, here's a general recipe. First, you must impoverish your reality by removing all distractions and limit your awareness to a single, or at most a very few objects of attention. This narrowing of attention can be helped along by the passions inspired by drugs, trauma, by joining some religious or political movements or by staying at home and watching a lot of television or computer screen. It would be a good idea to get rid of distractions like kids, magazines or books — especially books that give you options or make you think about other possibilities. Second, you must convince yourself that all options — other than your chosen perfect ideal, of course — are "evil" and every attempt that your monkey mind makes to have variety must be crushed and that you must keep your mind "pure" and only allow thoughts about your chosen passion. This mental trick will serve to concentrate your attention firmly on the object of your monomania. A second order loop which reinforces or rewards your monomania in such a regular and consistent way that even pain does not deter you, will 'fix' your trance. You will then be entranced in a pathological trance.

While pathological trances are not at all desirable, most people nearly all of the time are either in a trance or are engaged in trying to get others into trance. It is precisely pathological trance, not the yogic trance, that permeates most of our waking reality. It seems to me that once we can identify these pathological trances on a personal level we can take steps to avoid them.

If trance is defined as fixated thinking, then nearly all human activities create some type of trance. The bounded circles of thinking that keep us in trances are countless. The entire "ordered universe" is a trance. But there is an escapists pleasure in remaining in trance and a deep human fear of the chaos which can result if there were no trance "order" to life.

Terminating Addictive Trances

Start at any place in your addictive trance. Addictive trances reward an impoverished thought-set. You can help reduce any addiction by *rewarding* the *enrichment* of your thoughts. This means to expand the variety of your thoughts without trying to remove the thoughts you think are the problem. Continue expanding and enriching your thoughts with new and stimulating ideas, people and experiences. When the variety of your thoughts becomes robust, ideas will be self-generating and the addictive trance will naturally cease to exist by definition.

One effective way is to find the trance generating loop and replace one element in that loop. Wait until the dissociated trance plane changes, then replace a second element. Continue until the second order dissociated trance plane is unstable enough so that you can attack the primary trance generating loop. Once you destroy the primary trance generating loop the addictive trance will stop.

Pathological Trance and Psychoses

Limited awareness, the special characteristic that identifies a dysfunctional, impoverished reality, also identifies a type of trance state that may be characteristic of a posthypnotic state. Certainly those who have delusions can be considered to be in a trance of some sort. But of what sort is it?

Compulsive repetition, memory defects leading to various types of amnesias, faulty registration and recall and reactive confabulations and misidentifications resulting in disorientation can suggest some schizophrenic psychoses or a variety of organic brain disorders or a pathological trance.

Even a neurotic's inability to abandon old and disadvantageous patterns of reacting can suggest that a repetitive and compulsive behavior is due to some type of pathological trance. That is, it may not be enough to point out or interpret unconscious mental contents without simultaneously investigating the possibility of trance generating loops, secondary trance generating loops and examining the nature of the dissociated trance planes and trance forces that are created by such loops.

It is known that simple and uncomplicated repetitive behavior can be terminated through vigorous stimulation except when there is a gross defect of attention. Trance, too, can be terminated, except when the dissociated trance plane contains secondary loops or when multiple dissociated trance planes exist whose combined trance force components exceed the energy available to the normal ego structure. In such cases, trance termination is very difficult.

Since, normally, trance reduces both body awareness, memory functions, judgement, etc. it is not at all desirable to indefinitely prolong trance or to create habitual trance states. To do so increases the potential that the body or ego structure becomes damaged and that subsequent action does not correspond to reality, i.e. becomes delusional. Although temporary trance states are in fact essential to an intelligent adaptation to life, prolonged trance produces a variety of effects some of which can be termed pathological but some others can be termed remarkable and extraordinary. Distinguishing between normal and pathological trance can be determined by measuring and analyzing the numbers and extent of dissociated trance planes and their associated trance force components relative to the normal ego structure and its energy needs.

Trance Analysis

How does this slightly abstract and mathematical theory become practical? When we are confronted with our own mental behavior or someone else's, we might want to determine if there is a trance, what kind of a trance it is and what kinds of characteristics the specific trance may have. You might want to change the trance in some ways. But before you can change a trance, you need to know how to recognize one.

In learning *trance analysis*, I suggest that you use yourself as the subject before attempting to use trance analysis on others. In this chapter I will give you several examples of ordinary trances and how they are created and changed.

Recognizing a Trance

Trance occurs partly as a natural result of a more efficient utilization of cognitive energy. A trance makes it easy for the brain to do multiple things at the same time and to do some of those things more efficiently. However, in doing multiple things simultaneously some things are done with different mental functions enabled or disabled. It is because some cognitive functions are disabled that trance seems scary to some people.

Some cognitive functions are always changed in a trance. By looking for these common changes in cognitive energy utilization we can become aware that a trance exists.

Characteristics of trance include the following: disabling of judgment, disabling or limiting of volition, decrease of body awareness including eye fixation and immobility, an increase in the vividness or number of visions or hallucinations, inability to perform some mental functions and increased ability to perform other functions. I do not want to imply that there is always an absolute*dis*abling of judgement, etc. There may also be an enabling of a more accurate or more perceptive judgement, for example. However, if a person is utilizing a specific level of judgement when not in a trance, then, that level is different in a trance; and, so far as it is different, the new level of judgement represents a disabling of judgement from the prior level. For example, a person may be incapable of performing mathematical calculations while in an ordinary state of awareness, but may perform mathematical calculations exceedingly well while in a trance. I would say that their *ordinary* mathematical capabilities have been *dis*abled while in trance, leaving the question as to what their mathematical capabilities are while in trance open.

These characteristics of trance might not be obvious if a person is in a deep trance. The reason is that when a person is familiar or habituated to trance, more conscious control is possible. The characteristics above must be thought of as indicative of trance.

My model for trance separates the cause of trance (trance generating loops) from the effects of trance. Because the model is both more abstract and more precise than a socio-psychological model, the word *trance* now must include a wider range of behaviors than when it specifically referred solely to a deep hypnotic trance, a medium's trance, a spiritualist trance and other types of trances. The word trance continues to include these exotic and deep hypnotic and mysterious trances, but explains and describes such trances as being dependent on certain conditions which have been described in the model.

From a diagnostic and analytical point of view, we can now take the characteristics of trance logic as being suggestive of the existence of trance. That is, to be more explicit, the necessary and sufficient condition for trance is the presence of a loop which produces the dissociative trance, and the dissociative trance causes the disabling of some cognitive functions. The disabling of some cognitive functions makes the appearance as trance logic. Therefore, the presence of trance logic is suggestive of the existence of dissociative trance, i.e. trance.

The following is a partial list of cognitive functions which have been shown to be mitigated by trance:

Memory

Memory is the ability to accurately recall an experience. When memory is disabled, accurate recall fails. When memory is partly disabled elements of remembered experience may be absent, reversed, or there may be new elements from associated experiences.

There may also be an enhanced recall of memories, including vivification.

Whenever memory is not accurate a trance may be presumed to exist in the absence of other compelling explanations such as organic diseases.

Hallucinations

When mental organizing functions are disabled, sensation may be organized around preexisting physical or subtle stimuli which may be subjectively perceived as fantasy, visions, daydreams, or hallucination.

Hallucinations are not necessarily the result of a pathological process. They may be also the result of a process which disables a gross socially acceptable cognitive process and enables more subtle cognitive processes which are not close to the statistical mean.

For example, when multiple dissociative trances have been created, hallucinations and vivid images and fantasies can readily be experienced. When ego awareness is established in one of the dissociated trance planes and the hallucinations of the second dissociated trance plane are 'remembered', then there is a type of reality which is imposed on the second dissociated trance plane. If one is experienced in trance, and the dissociated planes are nonaddictive, the reality of these hallucinations are never believed, but in addictive trances or in trances in which there are strong trance forces and well-established dissociated trance planes, I could imagine that the presence of such multiple dissociated trance planes would be experienced as frightening or confusing and a therapist would diagnose a person experiencing such multiple dissociated trance planes as exhibiting pathological delusions.

On the other hand, the mere existence of multiple dissociated trance planes with the presence of hallucination or vivid images may simply represent an enhanced subtle inner perception. In order to ascribe a meaning or association to hallucinated visions, it is necessary to watch the hallucinations for some time.

The presence of hallucinations is suggestive of trance, but hallucinations do not necessarily indicate pathological delusions except when a person is unaware of what is happening.

Inhibition of body movement
When there is less somatic awareness, there may be involuntary movements, or, in the absence of stimulation,

body movements will appear to be inhibited. Limb catelepsy is an example of this.

Trance may absorb the attention so strongly that somatic awareness is disabled. Limb anesthesia is an example of this.

When there is an inhibition of body movement, a rigidity in the limbs, or a lack of body awareness, a trance may be presumed.

Fixed attention

Likewise, when eye movement and attention is fixed, trance is presumptive. It is often the case that when the attention is inward eye fixation is a side-effect.

Lack of volition

When a person lacks volition or will, trance is suggested. Trance is a more efficient utilizer of energy, and therefore disables inefficient processes. One can always presume that there is a trance when the will is absent; however, the mere lack of volition does not give a clue, usually, as to what the trance is about.

Ability to learn

Some cognitive functions are either increased or decreased by trance. The ability to learn may be increased or decreased. A change in the ability to learn is suggestive of trance.

Inability to make critical judgements

When the ability to make critical judgements is inhibited, then trance may be presumed. When a population has an inability to make critical judgements with respect to their leaders or political representatives, a common trance is presumptive.

Self-observation

Self-observation is often enhanced in trance, owing to the dissociation and literalism. Self-observation is indicative of trance.

Dissociation

The subject will be dissociated in trance, but may or may not be aware of the fact of dissociation. Often, and because of a lack of training, when one becomes aware that one is dissociated, then the dissociation terminates. With training, it is possible to be aware that one is dissociated without terminating the trance.

One important characteristic of any trance is that it creates dissociation and thinking occurs in the dissociated trance plane.

Literalism

The literal interpretation of words is indicative of a trance. Lawyers, computer programmers and many bureaucrats often are literal in their interpretation of words. It would seem that this indicates a trance. A trance analyst would look for a trance generating loop.

Trance force (Weirdness)

When unusual or magical occurrences take place, or when there is a certain unusual atmosphere, or when there seems to be a particular compulsion to engage in a specific behavior, this *may* indicate that a strong trance force is present. Strong trance forces indicate either constructive trance generating loops such as posthypnotic suggestions are being carried out or that the effects of a well-established dissociated latent plane are being felt. If it can be established that the sensations are due to external causes, then a trance originating from some external source can be presumed. When, as is far more likely, the sensations are due to internal causes, then a hypnotic trance is likely and the presumed "trance force" is more likely to be an hallucination rather than an external trance force.

Determine the trance generating loops

Once it has been determined that a trance exists, the next step is to determine the trance generating loops: that is, attempt to answer the question: what are the cognitive loops which cause the dissociative trance?

Trance generating loops are not particularly easy to discover in some specific cases, but discovering them are critically important to understanding the nature of a trance.

Trance generating loops can come into existence, create a trance, change to another trance generating loop, modify or deepen the trance and then change again. Trance generating loops can change quite rapidly. Each change will also change the dissociated trance plane. Because of this rapidly changing aspect, it can be difficult to perceive or to record the trance generating loops in one session. However, with patient observation an analyst can determine the major loops.

There is often one trance generating loop in simple trances. However, deep trances always have secondary order trance generating loops and they may be complex because of multiple changes in the underlying trance generating loops.

Primary Order Trance Generating Loop

In certain cases thoughts repeat in loop patterns. These looping patterns are important for learning and abstraction. The looping patterns of awareness generate secondary awareness planes which for the most part lie coincident to and within the cognitive plane. Trance generating loops do not need to be verbal thoughts. Some loops are mantras, drumming, pacing and leading for an hypnotic induction, the stimulus and response of television viewing and addictive behavior. The content of the loop is not necessarily a factor in generating secondary awareness planes, although it could be. The critical aspect is the repeating pattern which is the necessary and sufficient condition.

With increasing number of times a loop is repeated, as well as other conditions, these secondary awareness planes may split off or dissociate from the cognitive plane. This is quite normal and happens when something is 'learned'. It is the normal 'multiprocessing' aspect of thinking. In this process, for energy conservation reasons, some cognitive functions are disabled. The resulting awareness when these cognitive functions are disabled has been characterized as trance awareness, and this is defined as the 'dissociated plane.'

First order trance generating loops are often the patterns developed in early childhood.

Secondary Order Trance Generating Loop

A secondary order trance generating loop is a loop which promotes the continuation of the first order trance generating loop. For example, a hypnotist may give suggestions which promote relaxation and the deepening of a trance. Such suggestions, coming as they do within the dissociated consciousness (dissociated trance plane) of the subject represent a loop from the dissociated trance plane to the first order trance generating loop which may be, for example, the subject progressively relaxing as the voice of the hypnotist is heard. The progressively relaxed state of the subject promotes the continuation of the dissociated trance plane. If this secondary order trance generating loop persists long enough, a secondary dissociated trance plane will be created. When the secondary dissociated trance plane is created and can be sustained, then the subject is in a deep trance.

In a traditional hypnotic induction, it is the repeated words "You are becoming sleepy and relaxed" which induce a dissociated trance state. In the dissociated trance state the subject uncritically hears the words and it is the fact of being cognitively disabled that allows the subject to become sleepy and relaxed. This is trance abuse; that is, purposefully creating a disabled state and then taking advantage of it. What is important to realize is that it is the repetition alone which induces the dissociated trance state, and no other condition. The content about getting "sleepy and relaxed" has absolutely nothing to do with the creation of the dissociated trance state.

Chanting

Chanting is defined as the rhythmic repetition of words or sounds and includes singing and the recitation of poetry.

Because chanting involves voicing sound, it is somatic and aural.

Because chanting is a repetition of elements, the elements (words) can be counted and they belong to a limited set. The words are the trance generating loop.

When the chant is learned, and repeated several times, consciousness dissociates into the automaton consciousness which repeats the chant and to a second awareness process. The automaton consciousness is cognitive disabled. The second awareness is somatic disabled so far as voicing sounds is concerned.

Part of the available somatic energy is used to maintain the chant, and part of the cognitive energy is used to maintain the automaton, the trance generating loop. The remaining somatic energy may become insufficient to maintain somatic awareness and some anesthesia may be present. The remaining cognitive energy may become insufficient to maintain some cognitive functions (such as attention and or judgement) and what may appear to be suggestibility may be present. If the content of the chant contains embedded hypnotic suggestions, in those cases that there is a disabling of judgement and volition there will be an increase in the trance force with the result that the hypnotic suggestions will be carried out.

Let's look at a couple of other ways chanting induces trance. The Greeks used a rhetorical device called *epanodos* which means "the road back." With epanados the pattern to say is: "*a* is *b* and *b* is *a*" like Shakespere's "fair is foul and foul is fair." The trance generating loop is "Fair is foul." The second repetition of the trance generating loop is in a reverse order. The reverse trance generating loop is similar (and short) enough so that when the second reversed trance generating loop is completed a comparison with the primary residual awareness begins. "Comparison" in this instance is the beginning of multiprocessing. The residual awareness is larger in the reversed paradigm of epanados than the residual awareness of a simple multiple repetition of the trance generating loop, so epanados would be a relatively effective device for inducing trance.

Another Greek rhetorical device also effective for inducing trance is the *epistrophe*. In this paradigm a phrase ends with the same term. This paradigm can be used in a classical hypnotic induction, for example:

As you sit in the chair *you close your eyes*.

As you look at me *you close your eyes*.
As you relax deeper *you close your eyes*.
As you try to move *you close your eyes*.

The trance generating loop in this case is the repetition of a epistrophic pattern terminating with "you close your eyes." Again, as the mind hears one phrase similar to a prior phrase a mental comparison is made. The operation of memory in the comparison mode amplifies the residual awareness and causes dissociation. After some repetitions the awareness will be cognitive disabled in the dissociated trance plane in a trance and the trance generating loop will be "you close your eyes."

Most religious groups, from the Hari Krishnas to the Catholic, Buddhist, Jewish, Hindu and Muslim monks and devotees, all use chanting as part of their devotional practices. When it is understood how trances are generated, it may be realized that there is nothing magical in chanting. Nor is there anything significant or magical in the content or words of specific chants. Even when Indians chant for rain, if the chant loop is repeated enough times and if there is dissociation with a sufficiently strong trance force, it is possible that a strong potential for rain could be created.

Drumming

Drumming is defined as the rhythmic repetition of sounds on an instrument.

Because drumming involves making sound, it is somatic and aural.

Because drumming is a repetition of elements, the elements (beats) can be counted and they belong to a limited set. The beats are the trance generating loop.

When the drum beat is learned, consciousness dissociates into the automaton consciousness which repeats the beat and to a second awareness. The automaton consciousness is cognitive disabled. The second awareness is somatic disabled. Part of the available somatic energy is used to maintain the beat, and part of the cognitive energy is used to maintain the automaton. The remaining somatic energy may become insufficient to maintain somatic awareness and some anesthesia may be present. The remaining cognitive energy may become insufficient to maintain some cognitive functions (such as attention and or judgement) and what may appear to be suggestibility may be present.

Shamans, NewAge healers, witches and others often use drumming to create trance states. The effective use of drumming for trance would most likely involve rhythms which are attractive, which repeat, yet difficult to follow or to understand. Some rhythms are more effective than others. Some rhythms are more effective for some people than others.

Drumming, unless it is a single monotonous beat, consists of several trance generating loops. Each phrase of the drumming rhythm represents a single trance generating loop. In jazz drumming or reggae or in other genre, there are many trance generating loops. As one listens to one trance generating loop once or twice, there will be a dissociation. In the dissociated trance plane the awareness continues to listen to the drum beats but in a dissociated state. When awareness hears a second trance generating loop that too produces a dissociated trance plane slightly different than the first. As the jazz or reggae beat continues the awareness surfs along the changing dissociated trance planes. For each dissociated trance plane there is a corresponding trance force, and it is the combined trance forces of all the dissociated trance planes which gives pleasure.

Music

Music, or rather listening to music, is defined as the listening to a rhythmic repetition of notes or melody.

Listening to music involves an attention to sound.

Because music is a repetition of sound elements, the elements (sounds) can be counted and they belong to a limited set. The sound set is the trance generating loop.

When the music is heard sufficient times to become familiar, consciousness dissociates into the automaton consciousness which follows the sound and to a second awareness. The automaton consciousness is cognitive disabled. The second awareness is aurally disabled.

Part of the available somatic energy is used to maintain the attention on the sound, and part of the cognitive energy is used to maintain the automaton. The remaining somatic energy may become insufficient to maintain somatic awareness and some anesthesia may be present. The remaining cognitive energy may become insufficient to maintain some cognitive functions (such as attention and or judgement) and what may appear to be suggestibility may be present.

There can be no doubt that trances are induced by music of all kinds. The rhythms of the music need only be sufficiently charming to maintain interest and be pleasant enough to allow the listener to dissociate.

Each rhythm loop is a trance generating loop and so is each melody. As music is played, these multiple trance generating loops give rise to as many dissociated trance planes. When the dissociated trance planes are sufficiently coincident to each other, the trance force will come into existence and the music will have a trance effect. If the music creates non-coincident dissociated trance planes the trance force will be weak, and there will be a tendency for the trance to break.

Marching

Marching is defined as the rhythmic repetition of steps.

Because marching involves movement, it is somatic.

Because marching is a repetition of elements, the elements (movements) can be counted and they belong to a limited set. The movements are the trance generating loop.

When the march is learned, consciousness dissociates into the automaton consciousness which repeats the movements and to a second awareness. The automaton consciousness is cognitive disabled. The second awareness is somatic disabled.

Part of the available somatic energy is used to maintain the march, and part of the cognitive energy is used to maintain the automaton. The remaining somatic energy may become insufficient to maintain somatic awareness and some anesthesia may be present. The remaining cognitive energy may become insufficient to maintain some cognitive functions (such as attention and or judgement) and what may appear to be suggestibility may be present.

Marching is a powerful trance inducer. By combining marching with music and rhythmic drumming along with the simultaneous delivery of repeated hypnotic suggestions as part of a marching chant, or suggestions given by the drill master, it is possible to create highly motivated armies without personal feelings.

Dancing

Dancing is defined as the rhythmic repetition of steps.

Because dancing involves movement, it is somatic.

Because dancing is a repetition of elements, the elements (movements) can be counted and they belong to a limited set. The movements are the trance generating loop.

When the dance is learned, consciousness dissociates into the automaton consciousness which repeats the movements and to a second awareness. The automaton consciousness is cognitive disabled. The second awareness is somatic disabled.

Part of the available somatic energy is used to maintain the dance, and part of the cognitive energy is used to maintain the automaton. The remaining somatic energy may become insufficient to maintain somatic awareness and some anesthesia may be present. The remaining cognitive energy may become insufficient to maintain some cognitive functions (such as attention and or judgement) and what may appear to be suggestibility may be present.

Dancing combined with appropriate hypnotic suggestions and anchoring with somatic triggers can be used for creating love trances.

Triggers

When a trance generating loop is repeated for which there has been established a strong dissociated trance plane, that is, a dissociated trance plane with a trance force, then there is a strong tendency for the dissociated trance plane to be created whenever the trigger is invoked.

Many hypnotic inductions are done by the skillful use of triggers. NLP practitioners call these "anchors" when a somatic association is made to a dissociated state. Advertisers use musical jingles and visual anchors — such as company logos — to invoke brand recall and the subsequent product desire.

Complex Trance Generating Loops

A trance generating loop can be thought of as a repetition of words. And yet, each word also has a meaning. A word is also the result of an underlying learning process. For example, a trance generating loop can be: *I know my Mom really loves me.* This trance generating loop could conceivably be repeated by someone and repeated often enough will produce a trance. However, the word *Mom* is itself the trigger of an underlying trance generating loop. What does *Mom* mean? In order to answer this question, we would need to discover the underlying trance generating loop for Mom.

Characterize the Dissociated Trance Plane

It is important to assess the dimensions of the dissociated trance planes and to estimate the trance force which will certainly exist. There are two ways to estimate the dimensions of the dissociated trance plane. First, the possible content of the dissociated trance plane must be assessed; second, the boundary of the dissociated trance plane must be determined. The content of the dissociated trance plane includes that which results from additional perceptions, unusual abilities, or increased sensitivities. The boundary of the dissociated trance plane can be estimated by discovering what *cannot* be in the dissociated trance plane. By describing what is in the dissociated trance plane as well as what cannot be in the dissociated trance plane, an estimate of the dimensions can be made.

Trances always cause a limiting of attention. What attention is limited to is sometimes not the purpose of the trance. Often the purpose of a trance is to eliminate awareness. For this reason, it is important, when trance is presumed to exist, to examine and to enumerate whenever possible, what is being excluded from ego awareness.

Estimate the Trance Force

The trance force which is created by the dissociated trance plane is partially the result of cognitive energy conservation processes. For example, the dissociation which occurs in hand levitation frees some cognitive energy and this same energy is diverted into muscle movement and rigidity. It may be possible to measure components of the trance force by determining how much counterforce is needed to prevent hand levitation. The energy at which dissociation ceases would provide an approximate relative measure of some trance force components.

The trance force is present when there is any trance. That is, as soon as the dissociated trance plane comes into existence, then there is a trance force. The energy needed to break the trance is a measure of the trance force.

With a first order trance generating loop the trance forces are quite small. With second order trance generating loops there is a second dissociated trance plane and a second trance force which is due solely to the second dissociated trance plane. It is the combination of the first trance force with the second which provide a stabile trance and an order of magnitude increase in the trance force. When sustained or possibly in some ways modulated we postulate that the trance force can affect other biological and non-biological systems. The mechanism is not known how this occurs. There seem to be similarities between trance forces and electromagnetism in the sense that trance forces propagate somehow. If this is the case, then the trance forces would give rise to a new technology very similar to the technology which has arisen from Maxwell, Lorentz, Tesla and others.

Types of Trance

Because the primary induction process may occur either in the cognitive plane or in the dissociated plane and the subsequent perception may be focused on either internal or external processes, trances may be categorized into several major types, depending on the combination.

Ordinary thought objects are impulses in the brain which reflect in some sense the processes and sensations that occur in the body. No restrictions are placed on what a thought is nor what a sense is. The cognitive plane is the theoretical plane of awareness which is derived from thought objects.

When the number and strengths of the dissociated planes exceeds that of the primary cognitive awareness plane, the sense of self, the "I", switches to the dissociated trance plane, which is often called a *trance* state. Some cognitive functions when disabled exhibit 'trance logic'.

Sensations and mentations which occur in trance may occur either from external stimulation (voice, images which are seen, sensations which are felt by the body) or from internal stimulation (memories, voices, visions, feelings and emotions). These sensations may occur in either the cognitive plane or in the dissociated plane, and give rise to different types of trance. There are several types of trance which are implied by the model. Each type depends on the location of the trance generating loop and the location of the persons ego awareness.

Meditation Trance

The first type of trance is characterized by a generating loop in the cognitive plane with internal stimulation which is perceived from the dissociated plane. Meditation, mantra and inner visualizations are examples of this type of trance. One may call this the *meditation type trance*.

In order to induce a meditation trance all that is necessary is to repeat some sequence of sounds or a mantra or a trigger word mentally. After some time, there will be the subjective dissociated experience of what appears as ordinary thought while at the same time the mantra will be heard or experienced, possibly faintly or from far away. The duality of the subjective experience, that is of a repeating loop as well as apparently ordinary thoughts is a meditation trance. The apparently ordinary thoughts are actually occurring in the dissociated plane, so the thoughts are not ordinary. Some meditators if interrupted in this state experience a mild shock or involuntary reflex as the dissociated trance plane collapses.

There is a danger in meditation trance which may not be obvious, and I want to discuss that now.

Many meditation groups will begin a meditation silently, and then, at some point, the meditation leader will begin to speak. Sometimes the subject will be a prayer and sometimes it will be meditation instruction. Whenever you are meditating, all of your thoughts occur in the dissociated plane. Your ego consciousness is in the dissociated plane, and when a meditation leader speaks, the suggestions which are given have a hypnotic effect.

The meditation leader is inserting other sequences which will either destroy the dissociated trance plane or these sequences may change the dissociated trance plane. Perhaps you have had the following experience: you have been meditating with a group for thirty minutes or so and then the meditation leader begins to speak. You might have felt a jolt or shock as the dissociated trance plane collapsed, or you may not have been aware that the meditation leader spoke at all as you were so deep in the meditation trance, that is, your awareness was in the dissociated trance plane and some of your cognitive faculties were disabled. What did the meditation leader say to you? If the meditation leader was skilled in making hypnotic suggestions he could use the opportunity to program you in beneficial ways, ways that enabled you to gain more conscious control over the trance. On the other hand, if the meditation leader were unskilled, or had a hidden agenda, he might inadvertently make disturbing suggestions or suggestions which had the opposite effect, such as: "we are no longer tense and the sickness we feel has left our bodies," or "I let go and die for you, Lord God." Such suggestion are an abuse of trance. Because they are heard by the dissociated ego, some of your cognitive functions are disabled and all of the range of hypnotic effects can take place.

It may be for this reason that shamans and yogis prefer to meditate alone and far away from people. To be specific: the danger for you in meditating around people who talk to you is that what they say probably will have an hypnotic impact on you whether you agree with it, or like it or not. When someone speaks to you while you are meditating, the meditation trance easily becomes a hypnotic trance.

Specifically, to use trance theory to analyze the situation:

Meditation is a form of trance in which the dissociated ego awareness is in the dissociated trance plane. Some cognitive faculties are disabled. There is often a secondary order trance generating loop from the dissociated trance plane to the primary trance generating loop (the mantra or meditation task). Whenever anyone speaks to this dissociated ego, either:

1. The secondary order trance generating loop is interrupted.

2. The dissociated trance plane collapses.

3. The primary trance generating loop is interrupted by the insertion of the external voice.

or

1. The external voice is heard by the dissociated ego uncritically.

2. The dissociated trance plane is changes slightly due to the external voice.

3. A constructive trance generating loop is created by the changed dissociated trance plane. The constructive trance generating loop may become a 'posthypnotic' action, depending on the content of the external voice, the cognitive faculties that were disabled, the strength of the trance force and the content of the constructed trance generating loop.

That is, while meditation is a trance, it can very easily change to a hypnotic trance whenever someone begins to talk to you while you are meditating.

Because of the inherent dangers in hypnotic trances, I would suggest that whenever a meditation trance is desired, that there must be no external disturbance. Or, to put it in another way, if you are meditating and someone begins to speak with you, open your eyes and stop meditating. Unless, of course, you don't mind what they suggest.

If a meditation leader wishes to use trance theory to deepen and strengthen the meditation trance through a short term hypnotic procedure, then the first and last suggestions should be "continue meditating." Suggestions may be given to deepen the meditation trance by establishing secondary order trance generating loops over which the meditator has control. But I feel it is an abuse of the meditator for anyone to verbalize hypnotic suggestions.

Hypnotic Trance

The second type of trance is characterized by a generating loop in the cognitive plane with an external stimulation which is perceived from the dissociated plane. Hypnosis, television viewing, movies, music, driving a car, playing a drum are activities which are examples of this type of trance. In short, this is the *hypnotic trance.*

Traditional hypnotic trance induction used decades ago required the operator to repeat a formula or to make passes with the hands. Trance was induced by means of this secondary order trance generating loop and the dissociation of the subject occurred with the ego awareness moving in to the dissociated trance plane.

In general, hypnotic trances are quite dangerous if the content of the external stimulation is not controlled.

It is specifically because some cognitive functions are disabled that suggestions from external sources have their effect. Suggestions can alter the trance forces which have been generated by the energy changes in cognitive functioning. These trance forces will have far-reaching effects when the intensity of these forces is high.

Once it is realized how hypnotic trance is created and used, the answer to the frequently asked question: "Can you be made to do something against your will when you are in a hypnotic trance?" is yes. Those who say no either want to abuse you hypnotically or they don't know what they are doing.

Addictive Trance

The third type of trance is characterized by a generating loop in the dissociated plane with an external stimulation which is perceived from the dissociated plane. Addictions of all kinds are characteristic of this type of trance.

The main difference between a hypnotic trance and an addictive trance is in the location of the trance generating loop. Any inner repetitive process which takes place in a cognitive disabled dissociated plane (an unrealized unresolved emotional trauma, for example), and which is stimulated by or modulated by external triggers is an addictive type of trance. Hypnotic trances have their trance generating loops in the cognitive plane, but addictive trances have their loops in the dissociated plane.

In the beginning of this book, I mentioned that I was addicted to meditation. When one meditates, that is a meditation trance. When someone talks to you while you are in a meditation trance, it very quickly becomes a hypnotic trance. When you begin to mentally repeat the external stuff you heard while you are in a hypnotic trance, you begin to *believe*. And when you start to believe, then you go into a addictive trance which is addiction. This means that your primary trance generating loop is now in the dissociated plane, and your ego is also in the dissociated plane, and you will have much less contact with reality. In other words, you get stuck. In spite of the fact that addictive trance is fundamentally disabling such trances can seem very pleasurable. When a person is in a deep hypnotic trance with suggested anesthesia, a knife cut can be perceived as a pleasurable experience, when in fact it is damaging. When the generating loop is in the dissociated plane, as in an addictive trance, the knife cut can be experienced as a pleasure which it is desirable to reexperience.

Addictive trances are the posthypnotic types of trances where one can never get enough of the trance experience because fundamentally you are living in an hallucination. Addictive trances are the types of trances that consumers who watch a lot of television can be in. They are the compulsive shoppers for example. Perhaps they watch a lot of television and they have this urge to buy something; yet, the buying of it does not satisfy the urge so they buy some more. Basically, from a trance analysis point of view, the consumer is trying to fulfill the hallucination of a need. They are trying to shoot the hallucinated tiger with a real gun. That is, there really is no need, but the consumer, in this trance, hallucinates the need and tries to fulfill it by buying something. The trance generating loop occurs in the dissociated trance plane, but requires some external stimulation, like buying something, in order to complete the secondary trance generating loop.

Other types of addictions can be analyzed in the same way.

An alcoholic may have the following type of structure: the trance generating loop which occurs in the dissociated plane contains a painful idea or experience or hallucinated vision along with a denial of the painful idea connected with drinking alcohol. This loop occurs in the dissociated plane, that is, in a trance. The ego perceiving all this is in the dissociated plane which is created by this loop. Physically drinking alcohol helps reinforce the denial of pain. In fact, the inebriating effect of the alcohol creates both pain and its anesthetic denial of the pain. Thus, there is a connection between an external act (the drinking) and the content of the dissociated plane in which the trance generating loop exists. Other structures are possible, including multiple dissociated trance planes, and loops with other content as well as secondary loops.

Centric Trance

A fourth type of trance is characterized by a generating loop in the dissociated plane with an internal stimulation which is perceived from the dissociated plane. Centric trances contain multiple dissociated trance planes in some of which the trance generating loops are found. These types of trances are usually quite complex and often generate strong trance forces. Psychosis is sometimes characteristic of this type of trance. In general, a loop in the dissociated plane means a type of self-induced hypnosis is being created in which the ego awareness is totally involved. It is a trance full of illusions, delusions, and hallucinations. Body awareness is at a minimum and so may be compassion.

The nature of centric trances implies that strong trance forces are created. This is not to suggest that everyone run out and try to generate a centric trance, but the progressive training of the mind may enable some individuals to create strong centric trances which can be terminated at will.

Highly developed egos, driven individuals on a "mission," certain kinds of visionaries, artists, or self-proclaimed messiahs, etc. are likely to be in successful centric trances in which the trance forces are so intense that they sweep up others in their trance by potentiating dissociated trance planes and constructive trance generating loops, often over distances. Movie stars, gurus, saints and "Male chauvinist pigs" could all be thought to be in these centric types of trances, and there are others.

Summary of Trance Analysis

Mental phenomena can be analyzed in terms of trance.

In order to do trance analysis, the following steps should be taken.

1. On the most obvious level, the trance analyst must look for obvious signs of the presence of a trance. These have been enumerated above as characteristics of trance logic. These may be most obvious when deep trance exists as well as the perception of an intense trance force.

2. Once it has been determined that a trance (or trances) exist, the trance analyst must try to determine the underlying trance generating loops.

3. For each trance generating loop, the dissociated trance plane must be described. Especially, the duration and the boundary of the dissociated trance plane and a description of what is in the dissociated trance plane as well as what is specifically excluded.

4. For each dissociated trance plane there is associated a trance force. The strength or intensity, duration and effect of the trance force must be estimated and described.

5. Second order trance generating loops must also be described as well as the deep effects of any triggers within the loops.

6. Once the trance generating loops and dissociated trance planes are specified along with the trance forces then the type of trances are important to identify.

Being able to recognize a trance and to begin to discover some of the underlying characteristics will enable you to begin to change and to attempt to terminate some of the trances.

Contemporary Hypnosis and Trance Technology

Dissociation

There is actually nothing new about the concept of dissociation, which is defined as "the splitting off of certain mental processes from the main body of consciousness with various degrees of autonomy" (Hilgard, 1977, 1992). This definition, however, is too vague to be useful for describing trance. Specifically Hilgard's definition seems to circumscribe at least three types of distinct phenomena all of which could be termed "dissociation," but which are functionally different in important ways. The three types of dissociation are abstraction, autonomous multiprocessing and trance.

Dissociation generally is the mechanism by which mental processing becomes distributed to dominant and latent sequences. When both dominant and latent sequences are continuing at the same time, then there is parallel processing. The latent sequence becomes the trained automaton. Parallel information processing, with or without awareness, seems to be a fundamental, distinct and common type of dissociation. A common example of parallel information processing is when you are stirring a cup of coffee and looking around the room. This is not a trance. The dominant sequence is looking around the room and the latent sequence is stirring the coffee. It becomes an obvious trance when your attention becomes fixed on one spot, and becomes obviously deeper when you cannot stir your coffee.

Abstraction is another type of dissociation in which a symbol is used for a concept. The symbol is dominant and the concept is latent. Abstraction is a cognitive method of saving energy. It is not a trance. It can become a trance under certain conditions however. For example, the word 'table' is an abstraction for a certain class of objects. When the word *table* is repeated often enough, slowly and with such emphasis that access to the latent content becomes increasingly fascinating and absorbing, a trance is produced. Words with a rich latent content work better, but this example can show you that it is the process and not the word that produces the trance.

What distinguishes the dominant from the latent sequences of dissociation is the disabling or enabling of certain cognitive functions from the latent sequence.

To distinguish the above definition of dissociation from other ideas of dissociation, I would agree with Hilgard (1977) that dissociation is a normal aspect of information processing. I would not agree with Bartis and Zamansky (1986) that dissociation is an "inconsistency" between an individual's perception of an event and other concurrent behavioral and/ or cognitive aspects of the same event. I partially agree with Spiegel (1986) that dissociation is a condition in which specific subsets of material exclude other subsets of material from conscious awareness. I would agree with Berstein and Putnam (1986) that dissociation includes normal and abnormal experiences, but not that it was a continuum, and I would disagree wholeheartedly that dissociation itself is pathological.

Belief and Compliance

Wagstaff (Lynn and Rhue, 1992) suggested that it would be better to disregard all the standard references to "trance," "altered states" and so on and to explain the phenomenon of hypnosis from a social and psychological perspective. In Wagstaff's view hypnotic phenomena are better explained through the concepts of belief and compliance.

From my point of view, belief and compliance themselves can be explained as social phenomena which occur due to trance generating loops which occur over time and to the dissociative states which result whenever the collective latent sums of these trance generating loops gain enough energy to produce appearances seeming to be realities separate from the originating trance generating loops. The actual content of the trance generating loop in a hypnotic inductive situation (arm levitation, for example) is different from the content of a trance generating loop in a television commercial (brand recognition, purchase motivation, brand loyalty, for example), which is again different from the trance generating loops in religious, political or scientific activities. Yet, all trance generating loops have the potential, under certain conditions, of creating the appearance of a separate reality. In my opinion, it is not necessary to study arm levitation, brand loyalty, and nationalism as separate phenomena.

The question is not whether hypnosis exists. Hypnotic trance is a cognitive condition which has measurable physiological consequences (Kawano and others), although the techniques for measurement are only now being developed in a sophisticated manner. Hypnosis is also a phenomena which can be explained as a very specific type of trance within the suggested paradigm. However, the present paradigm also suggests that social psychological concepts such as belief, compliance, expectation and so on cannot be used as explanations for trance.

A belief, for example, occurs whenever a trance generating loop has sufficient energy to produce a dissociation and the appearance of a separate reality. Since a so-called hypnotic state is also the result of trance generating loops (induction) and the resulting dissociation, the concept of belief cannot logically be used to explain hypnosis since belief is itself another example of the same phenomenon. The same argument can be made for compliance.

There is no need to introduce more and more terms to describe trance and other altered states of consciousness. It is sufficient to use already known concepts such as thoughts, thought objects, awareness and dissociation, but to define them in such a way that they describe systems phenomena. A well-defined system model for trance can help to provide a unified theoretical paradigm for hypnosis. Whether the underlying terms and their phenomenological consequences can be accurately measured can be left for developing future technologies.

How professional hypnotists create trance

According to Hammond (1990), writing in the *Handbook of Hypnotic Suggestions and Metaphors* for the authoritative American Society of Clinical Hypnosis, these are the techniques which are used by professional hypnotists and clinical hypnotherapists to induce trance and how these specific techniques are viewed from a trance engineering perspective.

Create positive expectancy

Creating positive expectancy is what Wagstaff calls *compliance*. In general, a client who has a problem and who comes to a hypnotherapist for a solution to that problem already has agreed to be compliant and has a positive expectancy whether or not it is verbalized. The therapist has nothing to do with creating this positive expectancy; it is enough if the therapist doesn't blow it for the client by saying something stupid. Expectation has nothing to do with primary inductions and has nothing to do with secondary inductions. It is also possible to induce trance by creating negative expectancy. Therefore, positive expectancy is not a condition for trance for the client.

The autohypnosis of the therapist, however, will have subtle, yet powerful effects in creating trance. The autohypnosis of the therapist can potentiate dissociated trance planes and produce constructive trance generating loops in the client.

Creating an acceptance or yes-set

Limiting choice establishes an important condition for trance. When a client is seeking approval and acceptance, it is easy to utilize this desire to motivate a client to accept an impoverished reality set. This, however, is a form of trance abuse, in spite of the fact that the results of the trance may be laudable.

From the point of view of trance theory, it is not necessary to create either an acceptance or a yes-set or a rejection or a no-set; it is only necessary to limit choice. The requirement of acceptance or yes-set assumes that compliance is a condition for trance. This condition is limiting and unnecessary.

Erickson's principles of individualization and utilization

One example of Erickson's principle of individualization is the NLP technique of tailoring responses to correspond with a client's natural sense modalities (visual, auditory, kinesthetic, olfactory). This technique paces a client on a somatic level and represents a limitation of attention as well as the construction of a primary trance generating loop. This corresponds to all of the critical elements of trance creation.

Establish rapport and a cooperative relationship

This requirement for an hypnotic trance is nothing more than compliance and limiting attention. Compliance has nothing to do with trance -- unless you are a social psychologist -- but limiting attention does, if you are a trance engineer. The idea of rapport is the ideational, emotional and behavioral congruence between two people. Rapport suggests a mutual pacing or reflection resulting in feelings of closeness, comfort and safety. From a trance engineering point of view, rapport is the mutual pacing loop — it is a cybernetic loop — which produces congruence and the resulting rapport which is termed a cooperative or compliant relationship.

The cooperative relationship between the therapist and the client is more fully described by Gilligan. Rapport and the resulting cooperative or compliant relationship is more quickly developed by utilizing Erickson's principle of individualization and utilization. A trance engineer, however, would recognize that underneath these social psychological ideas of *cooperation, rapport* and *compliance* is the loop, the mutual pacing loop; it is nothing more than a human system cybernetic loop and is another specific example of a trance generating loop. It is the trance generating loop that is the necessary and sufficient condition for trance. All such loops limit attention by definition and when repeated often enough will induce trance.

Interactive trance and confirming the acceptability of suggestions

Tailoring suggestions to be congruent with a clients expectations is a form of pacing of a client and develops a limitation of attention as well as enables the construction of a primary trance generating loop. So long as limiting and repeating aspects are present, trance will be created.

The carrot principle

Linking a client's motivations with your own suggestions is a form of pacing of a client and develops a limitation of attention as well as enables the construction of a primary trance generating loop. So long as limiting and repeating aspects are present, trance will be created. I am repeating this because you are probably already in a trance.

The law of concentrated attention: repetition of suggestions

The repetition of suggestions will limit the attention and create the conditions for dissociation and trance. This is an important aspect of trance creation and maybe you should tell your friends what a great discovery this is.

You may get the idea by now that what is set forth as multiple principles in inducing hypnotic trance are actually — from a trance engineers point of view — mere variations on the same principle.

The law of dominant effect

Seeking to stir your powerful emotions and to connect hypnotic suggestions to them is a use of your memory and the use of residual awareness and prior existing triggers in order to create a trance. This is properly a type of secondary induction.

The law of parsimony

Trances are induced without reference to a clock or billing rates. The law of parsimony has nothing to do with trance. It has something to do with the effective use of a professional hypnotist's billable time.

The principle of interspersing and embedding suggestions

Making suggestions when judgement is disabled is trance abuse. For a list of phrases which can be used for embedded suggestions, see below. This principle has nothing to do with inducing trance either from a primary or secondary induction point of view, but is specifically a way of *exploiting* disabled cognitive functions during a trance which has already been established.

The principle of positive reinforcement

This is a form of pacing of a client and develops a limitation of attention as well as enables the construction of a primary trance generating loop.

The principle of positive suggestion

In a generative cognitive loop such as "I am not hungry" the word *not* often tends to be forgotten. The loop can easily become "I am hungry." Perhaps the reason for this is that the word *not* or *no* is a trigger for an often well established dissociation into a pain/pain-relieving trance. For this reason, behaviorists and those who wish to instill suggestions often rephrase negative suggestions into positive ones such as "I feel *really* satisfied." Trance theorists will immediately recognize that the *no* or *not* is a trigger word into a primary induction to a pain trance. Since this trance is a somatic no-no, the only suggestion left once good judgement is disabled is the positive one when the *not* is eliminated: "I am hungry." It is for this reason that suggestions are made from a positive point of view.

This principle is important for parents to implement. I wince whenever I hear a parent scream at a child: "Don't run into the street; you'll get hit by a car!"

The principle of successive approximations

The expectations of the hypnotherapists have nothing to do with trance induction unless the hypnotherapists are themselves in a trance.

The principle of trance ratifications

Trance ratification refers to the process of providing the client with an experience that verifies for the client that they have been in a hypnotic trance. Trance ratification is an attempt by the hypnotherapist to make a secondary trance generating loop. That is, the client makes a reality map from the dissociated plane to the suggestions of the hypnotist.

Some hypnotic experiences which can help a client realize that they have experienced or are experiencing a trance are:

1. Amnesia
2. Arm levitation. This is a classic.
3. Glove anesthesias or analgesia.
4. Ideomotor signaling. Raise your finger if you understand this point.
5. Limb catalepsy.
6. Limb heaviness.
7. Time distortion.

Although this so-called principle of trance ratification is effective in creating a secondary loop, trance ratification is only one example of creating secondary loops.

Timing of suggestions and depth of trance

When a trance has been established and some cognitive facilities have been disabled, hypnotherapists will consider it an opportune time to make suggestions. This is trance abuse, but it works.

Pacing

Pacing represents a type of generative cognitive loop which is effective for inducing trance. The loop is established in the head of the client, and is not only a social loop between the hypnotist and his subject.

NLP practitioners utilize somatic clues such as eye movement and verbal clues to indicate the most effective ways to pace a subject. While for NLP practitioners such clues may be effective indicators, pacing can be effective with *any* somatic clues. Thus, if every time a client blinked the therapist raised a finger while in conversation this type of pacing would also result in a trance generating loop. Typing somatic and other clues, that is, mapping a client's eye movement or an astrological aspect to a therapist's clinical response strategy, when consistent over time, will constitute an effective trance generating loop and induce trance in the client and often in the therapist, too.

Pacing is what the tiger does to the rabbit. The tiger watches the rabbit and moves in the same way and at the same time that the rabbit does. The rabbit doesn't feel that anything is unusual. Perhaps the rabbit is not even aware of the tiger who almost moves simultaneously with the rabbit's shadow. On a human scale, pacing is reflecting, mirroring or following the verbal, somatic and other clues of another person. It represents a type of loop and represents a limitation of attention and action. Pacing results in feelings of comfort and safety; it is rapport. When the tiger has paced the rabbit for some time the rabbit may remember that every time it moved, something in the shadows moved. Could it have been his mother? At this point, the rabbit is dissociated. Part of the awareness of the rabbit is remembering what happened in the past and observing the tiger to see if the tiger moves the way the rabbit's mother moves. The rabbit naturally moves towards safety, except now, because part of the cognitive functions of the rabbit are disabled, and anyway, the tiger seems to move also like a rabbit.

Leading and Embedded Commands

When the tiger jumps in such a way that leads the rabbit to jump into an unsafe place, the tiger jumps on the rabbit. Leading is what the tiger does to the rabbit after the tiger has paced the rabbit for some time. On a human scale, if one paces a person long enough, then it is possible to lead or to give a suggestion to the person and which the person will carry out. The reason this works is that pacing is a trance generating loop and when continued long enough always results in dissociation and the disabling of some cognitive functions. Once the cognitive functions are functions are disabled, then a command can be given which will be carried out often because judgement, etc. is disabled.

The following are 'truisms' which can be used to carry embedded commands. Embedded commands do not induce trance, but are forms of *trance abuse*; that is, they are ways to utilize the disabled cognition of the subject to gain acceptance of your horrible, immoral, indecent and exploitative suggestions, or the therapeutic, enlightening and relaxing ones. Embedded commands do not have anything to do with trance induction, *per se*, but the nature of the behaviors that embedded suggestions promote in subjects might properly be considered to be *compliance* by some psychologists.

The following is a rather long list, but it is important for you to understand that trance abuse can occur in a variety of ways. In the following sentences, you can substitute one of your favorite — but naughty — desires as the [command] to understand how trance abuse works in practical ways. Where [pace] is indicated, simply describe the person you are talking to, such as 'You are sitting there' or 'You are smiling now' and so on.

1. [command] in a way that meets your needs.
2. Someone once told me, [command]
3. Someone said, [command]
4. A person could, [name], [command]
5. A person is able to [command]
6. A person may [command], because [any reason]
7. A person may not know if [command]
8. A person might, [name], [command]
9. After [pace] you can [command]
10. All that really matters [command]
11. All that's really important [command]
12. Almost as though [command]
13. And as [pace] occurs, [command] may occur more than you'd expect.
14. And do you notice the beginning of [command]?
15. And if you wish [command]
16. And it appears already that [command]
17. And maybe you'll enjoy noticing [command]
18. And when you [pace], you'll [command]
19. And would you be willing to experience [command]?
20. And would you like to [command]
21. And you begin to wonder when [command]
22. And you can be pleased [command]
23. And you can wonder [command]
24. And you can wonder what [command]
25. And you will be surprised at [command]
26. And, in an interesting way, you'll discover [command]
27. Are you aware of [command]

28. As soon as [pace], then [command]
29. As you feel [pace] you recognize [command]
30. Almost as if ..
31. At first [pace], but later [command]
32. At times like this, some people enjoy [command]
33. Can you [command]
34. Can you imagine [command]?
35. Can you notice [command]?
36. Can you really enjoy [command]?
37. Do you [command]
38. Does [command]
39. Don't [command] too quickly.
40. Don't [command] until you [command]
41. Eventually [command]
42. Everybody [command]
43. Everyone [command]
44. Give yourself the opportunity to see if [command]
45. How would it feel if you [command]?
46. I could tell you that [command] but [command]
47. I don't know if [command]
48. I wonder if you'd like to enjoy [command]
49. I wonder if you'll be pleased to notice [command]
50. I wonder if you'll be reminded [command]
51. I wonder if you've ever noticed [command]
52. I wouldn't tell you to [command], because [pace]
53. I'd like you to begin allowing [command]
54. I'm wonder if [command]
55. I'm wondering if you'll [command], [name] or not.
56. If you [pace], then [command]
57. In all probability [command]
58. In every culture [command]
59. Is isn't important [command]

60. It gives everyone a sense of pleasure to [command]
61. It is a very common experience to [command]
62. It isn't necessary to [command]
63. It may be that you'll enjoy [command]
64. It may be that you're already aware of [command]
65. It's easy to [command], is it not?
66. It's so nice to know [command]
67. Just allow it to happen [command]
68. Kind of like [command]
69. Maybe it will surprise you to notice that [command]
70. Maybe you haven't [command], yet.
71. Maybe you'll
72. Most of us [command]
73. Most people [command]
74. One can [name], [command]
75. One could [command], because [pace]
76. One doesn't have to, [name], [command]
77. One may, [name], [command]
78. One might, you know, [command]
79. People can, you know, [command]
80. People don't have to, [name], [command]
81. Perhaps beginning to notice [command]
82. Perhaps noticing [command]
83. Perhaps you are [command]
84. So that it's almost as if [command]
85. Some people [command]
86. Sometime [command]
87. Sooner or later [command]
88. Sooner or later, everyone [command]
89. The closer you get to [command] the more you can [command]
90. The feeling of [pace] will allow you to [command]

91. There was a time when you didn't [command]
92. Try to resist [command]
93. Very likely [command]
94. What happens when you [command]?
95. When you [pace] please [command]
96. When you [pace], then [command]
97. While you [pace] you can [command]
98. Why don't you [command] before you [pace]
99. Will [command]
100. Will you [command] now, or will you [command]?
101. Will you [command], or [command], or [command]?
102. With your permission [command]
103. Without knowing it, you've [command]
104. Without really trying, it will just happen all by itself [command]
105. You already know [command]
106. You already know how to [command]
107. You are able to [command]
108. You can [command], because [command]
109. You can [command], can you not?
110. You could [command]
111. You don't have to [command]
112. You don't need to be concerned if [command]
113. You may [command]
114. You may not know if [command]
115. You may or may not [command]
116. You might [command]
117. You might not have noticed [command]
118. You might notice how good [command] feels, when you [command]
119. You might notice the feelings [name] as you [command]
120. You might notice the sensations in [pace] while you

[command]
121. You might want to [command], [command] now.
122. You probably already know [command]
123. You won't [command] until [command]
124. You've known all along how to [command]
125. [pace], [pace], [pace], and [command]

All of the above statements are used by hypnotherapists in order to embed commands which may not be noticed by a person whose attention is not specifically attuned to the possibility that commands can be suggested through the use of these phrases. This type of manipulation is also trance abuse.

If a hypnotherapist simply uses these forms without a subject being dissociated the subject will, like the old rabbit, realize that the shadow contains a tiger. These forms are effective only as delivery systems.

All of these subtle and not-so-subtle suggestions do not have much to do with *inducing* trance as I have defined it, unless these suggestions were repeated. If the subject is already dissociated and partly disabled the above paradigms can be efficient methods of delivering suggestions. Because these suggestions and manipulations don't have much to do with inducing trance as I have defined it, one could almost agree with Wagstaff that compliance and belief have a lot to do with hypnosis, if it exists at all. And if the above suggestions were somehow identified as being important for *inducing* hypnotic trance, I would have to agree with Wagstaff that a *belief* in hypnosis has a lot to do with a *belief* in leprechauns and *compliance* is a condition for *inducing* trance.

Magic and Trance Technology

Reorientation

There is a lot of work to do in order to put what is already known about trance and how it is currently used into the categories of the model so that it can be used as a technology. In order to reorient you to this perspective, I will present ways to induce trance and give examples. In addition, I will make comparisons to what now exists and explain what is being done from my perspective.

The application of the principles of trance theory will probably be most productive and effective in hypnosis, hypnotherapy, meditation, religious rituals and magic, shamanistic practices, research in altered states of consciousness, and in possibly understanding and treating difficult 'trancelike' pathologies such as addictions and some delusional psychoses.

To make the bridge from magic to technology is a considerable amount of work. If there is no resistance to applying a technological technique to something as personal as religious ritual, then the possibilities of more effective religious ritual can increase. When a person does not have a vested, personal, emotional or private interest in maintaining their own ideas about magic or shamanism, it is more likely that the idea of making magic into a technology will be well accepted as an exciting possibility full of promise.

In either case, understanding how trance works and then practicing some of the techniques is the best way to start.

Inducing Trance

The following describes techniques to induce trance by promoting or setting the conditions to enable dissociation.

The first technique always uses a repeated set of stimuli in order to create the condition for dissociation. This will fit with the description in Chapter 3. Japa meditation, chanting, trance music, and repeated somatic acts are all primary inductions. Primary inductions always create triggers which can be later used in secondary inductions. A pure primary induction always uses a repeated set of stimuli which are not triggers. However, primary inductions always create triggers which can give a name to the residual awareness components of the trance. It is important to identify these triggers. This will enable a more rapid creation of trance in the future. In general, being able to create and establish trance only takes time. Some people take a bit longer, some a bit shorter, but eventually, with the establishment of triggers, all go into trance.

Secondary inductions use the triggers that have been established by primary inductions. Under the proper conditions, a trigger will potentiate or construct representations of the original set of stimuli and potentiate the trance. These are the techniques that advertisers use to induce light trances. Some marketing techniques refer to *hot buttons*, which consist of words like *deserve, remember, imagine*, etc. Such words trigger inner processes and potentiate dissociation. These hot buttons, when used, are called *secondary inductions*. Words which evoke visual memories are also triggers and effective for many people. Metaphorical hypnotic techniques use primarily secondary inductions because the metaphores evoke inner processes which are often triggers for trances.

Somatic triggers also work. The skillful use of triggers alone is sufficient to create trance. All hypnotic inductions use a combination of triggers and repetition in order to create the dissociated trance plane. Once the dissociated trance plane is created, then one must establish secondary trance generating loops in order to stabilize the dissociated trance plane.

Primary Inductions

Primary inductions use a trance generating loop to produce a pure dissociation rather than accessing triggers. Triggers, such as are used in NLP, and by advertisers, will, of course, work, but triggers always carry the associations of the underlying trance generating loops. These underlying loops can create alternative and undesirable dissociated trance planes.

Secondary Inductions

The use of triggers in order to invoke prior trance states must be done with some trance analysis beforehand. Although if it is simply desired to disable the critical judgement of a person before abusing them, triggers will be mostly be sufficient.

Emotional trigger words are often used by some advertisers, political and religious groups in order to perform a type of trance abuse that is tantamount to rape, but cannot be justified by arguing that the subject is voluntarily 'compliant'.

Secondary inductions are used in NLP and in many so-called consciousness-raising activities which really are not consciousness-raising at all, but are merely methods for disabling critical judgement. This enables the skillful operator to make suggestions of miracles quite easily.

Meditation Techniques

Inducing a meditation trance is something you must do yourself. That is, the limitation of attention and the repetition of a sequence (it need not be a mantra) are the only critical conditions. What is important is to be able to distinguish between a meditation trance -- which is a technique you do yourself, and a hypnotic trance -- which is a technique someone does for you.

In many traditions, a meditation student is first induced into a hypnotic trance by a meditation teacher. This hypnotic induction takes place during instruction or initiation or religious training or through a performance of ritual magic. It need not be so, but generally it is this way. The purpose of the hypnotic trance is to give a student the experience of trance, and, in so doing, explicitly instruct the student on methods that are effective in recreating that same or a similar trance. It may be that because of traditions of secrecy and because of a lack of knowledge of the technology of trance, various extraneous symbols and practices were attached to religious meditation practices. It could be for this reason that meditation techniques are often identified with some specific religious practice. In addition, the mantras or zikhr or holy prayers which are used as part of the trance generating loop are triggers to prior ideas or concepts or to emotionally heavy events. Mantra triggers to emotionally heavy memories will tend to engage a person on internal mental thoughts, visions and memories. ("Jesus died for your sins!") These types of mantra triggers make it relatively easy to establish trance in those persons who are easily drawn into such internal processes. When such mantras are chosen, it becomes especially easy to establish addictive trances. With a lot of practice, devotion and anchored somatic secondary trance generating loops these religious addictive trances can become centric with a rich range of potentially delusional ideas. You can find your own examples.

Autogenic training or self-hypnosis in which the primary responsibility remains with the solitary practitioner is probably a safer way to self-induce meditation trance. When groups of practitioners of meditation trance come together to enjoy a group meditation, one should be alert of the potential for a meditation trance to basically degrade into a hypnotic trance, and with the concomitant possibilities of trance abuse taking place.

One specific technique for meditation trance induction goes like this: Use the mantra *Shirim*. Close your eyes, wait about a half a minute, then start thinking the mantra over and over again. Eventually you will be bored and may even forget to repeat the mantra. This means that the residual awareness in the dissociated plane is of a higher energy than the trance generating loop which consists of the mantra. When you are aware that you have forgotten to repeat the mantra, remember to go back to the mantra. This sets up a secondary trance generating loop from the dissociated plane to the primary trance generating loop.

Another important point is to *remember* the mantra rather than repeating it clearly. Remembering the mantra invokes the residual awareness component, and this will help you to remain in the dissociated trance plane. *Hearing* the mantra faintly is also a technique for retaining the dissociative state.

Thoughts which occur do so while you are in a dissociated state. Never think you are 'just thinking' or that your consciousness is 'normal.' It's not. You are dissociated, and therefore some of your cognitive faculties are disabled.

Mantras are not the only vehicles for inducing a meditation

trance. However, if you would like a list of mantras to use, you can use any of the following, and there are many, many more from the religious and nonreligious traditions of the world (gathered from public sources):

Eng, Em, Enga, Aing, Aim, Ainga, Aima, Shiring, Shirim, Hiring, Hirim, Kiring, Kirim, Sham, Shama, Ing, Im, Shiama, Om Mane Padme Hum, Ya Ali, Hu, Hare Kali Om, Jai Ram, Hare Om, Om Nama Shivaya, Yaweh, Shri Shri Aing Aing Namah Namah, Money, Love, Sex, Health, Happiness, Power, Peace.

Other techniques of meditation, such as a visualization, will also be effective. You can actively visualize a face or a symbol (a circle, a cross, a star, the number 9, the mantra Hu) and when the symbol fades and you become aware that it has faded, you reconstruct it again mentally. This is basically the same form as the technique described above. Again, the trance generating loop does not need to be a mantra or a visualization and the actual content of the loop does not need to be religious. It can also be political, or emotional or financial.

Besides using any of the five senses as vehicles for the trance generating loop, you can also use somatic awareness such as watching your own breath. This technique is popular among Buddhists, for example. Again, the trance generating loop is the breath itself: the inhalation, the retention, the exhalation. The dissociated trance plane occurs when you forget to watch your breath. Then you should *remember* to *watch* your breathing. This will establish the secondary trance generating loop.

Other meditation trance techniques involve what might be called 'movement of awareness' in which you place your inner awareness on the chakras and move this awareness from chakra to chakra. As you do this, you can associate a mantra with each chakra, a color, a smell, and so on. You may integrate a particular body movement with your inner awareness as it moves along your spine or throughout the far reaches of the cosmos. Elaborate meditation trance techniques such as these are popular among the Tibetans and were practiced by ancient civilizations. Again, the trance generating loop in this technique is each point of your awareness. The content is not so important, but the fact that it is repeated is critical. What is important about content is to realize that when the dissociation occurs, the content will act as a suggestion. The suggestion may not be verbal, but will have some effect on the potentiation of the trance force.

Improving your trance

Strong trance forces result in both the possibility of perception of subtle processes and the potential for action at a distance and changes in remote processes. For most people, this characteristic action of strongly potentiated trance forces is the same as magic. Potentiating your trance force is critical for increasing your magical powers, if that is what you want to do.

For most people it simply is not possible to create these strong trance forces. Creating strong trance forces require the personal ability to sustain a strong dissociated trance plane and to *act* while in a deep trance. For many people, as soon as they are aware that they are dissociated and in a trance, the trance terminates. Channellers and healers are two groups who presumably can maintain their trance and move. People who manage to create centric trances can act while in a deep trance. However, such people may or may not have a good grip on reality; that is, they might be delusional psychopaths.

Some buyer's caution is advised; your mileage may vary.

Perhaps one of the reasons drugs are so desirable by many people is that drugs can help to maintain the dissociated state. Music, especially drumming, also helps to maintain the dissociated state through its repetitions of melodies and rhythms. However, the unfortunate fact is that music and drugs create hypnotic trances and not meditative trances. Therefore what is created is more likely to be hallucination rather than the strong trance forces associated with magic. The other problem with the use of drugs to enhance altered states is that drugs do not allow you to develop the conscious skills you need in order to control the trance force. In order to control the trance force you need to be able to do it yourself, without any external help at all and you certainly do not need to deal with interfering drug induced hallucinations.

A person who wishes to sustain a strong trance force must be fully capable of entering into meditation trance where the dissociated trance plane is stabile and the shape can be modified at will. This means that conscious control over the dissociated trance plane is required. Secondary order trance generating loops might be necessary at the beginning, but full conscious control requires that no secondary order trance generating loops be present.

Here is one way to develop strong trance forces.

1. Establish a meditation trance.

2. Stabilize the dissociated trance plane and deepen the trance with a secondary trance generating loop.

3. Keep your ego awareness in the secondary order dissociated trance plane. Practice changing the shape of the primary dissociated trance plane by changing the secondary trance generating loop. Then remove the secondary order trance generating loop and merge your ego back onto the

primary dissociated trance plane.

4. The merging of the ego awareness in the primary dissociated trance plane must not break the trance.

For many people, as soon as they become aware that they are in a trance, they come out of the trance. Or, if they are aware that they are in trance they can't do anything. Or, as soon as a deep trance is fully developed they become unconscious. These and other problems prevent most people from developing any controllable trance force.

In order to create trances with a strong trance force component, second order trance generating loops are necessary at the beginning. This means, practically, that within the dissociated trance plane an effort must be made to continue the trance generating loop. In meditation practices this is often the case since instructions are often given that "as soon as you are aware of your thoughts, easily go back to the mantra". Basically it means that no matter in what mental state you find yourself, even if most of your normal cognitive faculties are disabled, you must continue to do the process which caused the primary dissociation. This creates a secondary order trance generating loop. At this point, do not modify the primary trance generating loop. Just continue for a sufficiently long time so that the dissociated trance plane is well established. The primary trance generating loop adds a component of the trance force, and the secondary order trance generating loop will also add a component of the trance force. The primary dissociated trance plane will become quite stabile at that point that the secondary order dissociated trance plane becomes established. You will then be in a deep trance.

In order to make this clear, I will discuss the same strengthening of a trance from the point of view of the other three types of trance.

Meditation trances can be strengthened with the use of secondary order trance generating loops. Hypnotic trances can be strengthened by choosing the appropriate external stimulation to deepen the trance. The key word here is *appropriate*. How can you know that what your meditation guru says to you while you are in a deep meditation trance is really appropriate for your set of mental associations? Addictive trances can be strengthened by putting the ego on the secondary order trance generating loop and use any primary trigger to reinforce the secondary order trance generating loop. That means that you would rather meditate than do the dishes or win the lottery. Centric trances use any change in the dissociated trance plane to strengthen or reinforce the secondary order trance generating loop. Secondary trance generating loops tend to lock in the first order trance generating loops. When strong trance forces are present, you can be sure you are dealing with a person in one or more deep trances. Psychotics, addicts and religious zealots are often in these types of deep trances. Secondary order trance generating loops are often are connected with the motivations to perform stress-related behaviors.

For an addict, it means that whatever the causative substance or process, the dissociated state which is produced always results in doing more of the drug, alcohol or behavior which is at the root of the addiction. This secondary trance generating loop will fix the addiction rather well, but the effect of the drug or alcohol will tend to destroy the ego awareness.

For a centric trance, it means that the dissociated state produces more of the same type of behavior which was at the cause of the dissociation. Persons who are in centric trances are very difficult to deal with. They have their own realities, vivid hallucinations which are to them indistinguishable from reality. You could call them saints, or maniacs. The trance forces which they create are in general potentially quite impressive.

For a witch, the result of a magical rituals which were conducted within the circle should be causative to creating the same conditions which gave rise to the magical circle. The secondary order trance which results over time should help to transform the witch and increase the trance force considerably.

What is also important for a witch or magician or others who work with trance forces to be aware of is a strong grounding of the ego structure in meditation trance is critical to prevent loss of energy through the inadvertent creation of hypnotic or addictive trances. Such trances may 'feel good' but they dissipate the trance force.

If you wish to become effective with magic, you must be able to create and sustain intense centric trances, and to use them without any delusions at all. Centric trances create full realities, therefore there is quite a temptation to lose yourself in these false realities.

Most 'pretend' witches will be in hypnotic trance or addictive trances (or even disabling centric trance), and the trance force will be spent in disabling hypnotic or addictive processes. This means that the trance force will not function according to any 'will' of the witch, except perhaps to create rather vivid and believable hallucinations, i.e. delusions.

It is quite important for groups of witches or magicians to develop meditative trances individually first, such that there is at least one strong trance force in the group which can carry any weaker individuals. It would also be important — from a trance theoretic point of view — not to verbalize too much while in a circle. Such verbalizations will always disturb the dissociated trance planes and create other types of trances. The effect of such secondary trances will decrease or corrupt the trance force. There is a great tendency to elaborate rituals in the new goddess devotions, but from a trance point of view, these verbalized rituals always become hypnotic trances and can even become addictive trances. It is very important to use good trance engineering practices when making new rituals for magical purposes.

Groups which are interested in creating strong trance forces, must first establish strong trance forces by means of meditative trance on an individual basis. If this is not done, it is nearly almost certain that the trance forces will be diminished and that the meditative trance will degrade to a hypnotic trance. Groups in a meditative trance which expose themselves to the machinations of individuals who are in a centric trance risk the conversion of their meditation trances to group hypnotic, addictive, or, in some cases, disturbed and delusional psychotic trances. This phenomenon is found mostly in cults, but also in political movements.

For a shaman, the use of plants or substances to give rise to sensitivities to elemental plant and extraterrestrial energies should be causative to creating the same conditions which gave rise to the use of plants or substances and the encounters with other life forms. The secondary order dissociation which results over time should transform the shaman and increase the trance force to a high degree of empathy and understanding of alien entities and energies.

Most of the trances which are invoked by those who wish to enable the trance force will probably create hypnotic and addictive types of trances. These types of trances are not at all effective for the work of authentic witches or shamans or magicians, but these will be the most common trances created.

Primarily what is produced is hallucination.

In order to avoid producing hypnotic and addictive trances, it is critical to establish meditative trances first and to build the trance force independently over a long period of time. If there must be external stimulation of the dissociated ego, then the stimulation should preferably be free of content. That means music or drumming — without words — is probably one safe way. If secondary trance generating loops are intended to strengthen the trance forces, then considerable care in the design should be taken so that they can be removed. Preferably a complete trance analysis should be undertaken first in order to determine the depth and range of any triggers within the trance generating loops.

Most people cannot sustain even a simple dissociated state consistently enough or long enough to produce any trance force at all. It is for this simple reason that there are few real magicians or yogis in this world. The rarity of strong trance forces probably have a lot to do with the false idea that hypnosis doesn't exist. The fact is, that a significantly strong trance force is fairly rare. It can and does occur in deep trance states such as may be produced by deep hypnosis, long and deep meditation, and even by certain types of addictions and psychosis. There are charismatic centrics who seem to be quite lucky, but actually it is rather their highly developed trance force which works for them, or, we may also say, sometimes against them.

Centric trances are shared by both psychotic people (people with a destroyed ego structure, i.e. can't decide which dissociated reality is the real one) and by gurus, shamans, saints and masters, (who mostly do not have a destroyed ego structure) and also some very egocentric people (who have chosen one of the dissociated realities as the real one - and maybe they are wrong) found in the movie industry and 'male-macho-pig' types. Centric trances create strong trance forces, and they are beyond being addictive trances. People in centric trances certainly can do math, ride a bicycle, perform healings, murder people, and even hear voices talking to them from outside their heads (psychotics have this skill, and so did some people mentioned prominently in some religious books).

Becoming aware in the dissociated trance plane

One way to become aware in the dissociated trance plane is to watch yourself as you go into a trance and to observe the change in the dissociated trance plane and what happens to any change in the trance force. To do this, you can do this simple experiment.

Next time you are walking down the street, let your awareness be on your feet, one after the other. After a few steps, because this repetition is so familiar with most people, you will almost immediately begin to dissociate or to think of other things. There is a difference between your awareness in walking down the street and your awareness when you are thinking other thoughts. What you should become aware of is how your awareness is different, what cognitive functions are disabled and what energy has increased at the moment you have switched your thoughts from the awareness of walking to thinking of other things. This, and many other exercises, is what I did in order to become aware of trance and the effects of trance. There are many exercises along these lines in almost every meditation tradition.

The thinking of other thoughts always occurs in a trance; although you might argue that you are perfectly conscious, there is always some cognitive disabling, and, in fact, your awareness is smaller, but the trance force has increased (slightly). What is important is to develop this secondary dissociated awareness so that you can observe this change in awareness as you go into trance. This secondary dissociated awareness is like a witness, and it is this witness that you need to bring to life and stabilize, if you wish to control the created trance force.

With practice, and as you are able to sustain this witness consciousness, you may be able to understand the relationship between the shape of the dissociated trance plane and the trance force.

As I mentioned at the beginning of this book, maybe this is all quite well known and well understood somewhere; but although I have searched, I have not found anything which describes trance in this way.

Designing a trance

From a purely theoretical point of view, trance does not depend on the content of the trance generating loop. However, the triggers of important and powerful trance generating loops become like mantras in the sense that the triggers can evoke instant dissociation and strong trance forces.

In addition, once a person is in a trance, the content of the trance generating loop can act in a hypnotic way.

Many years ago there existed the idea that if you said to yourself: *Every day in every way I am getting better and better* then sooner or later you would. From the point of view of designing a trance, this probably even works. Repetition of the idea causes dissociation. The mind in the dissociated trance has partially disabled cognition. Continuing to repeat the trance generating loop would act as a suggestion to a hypnotic trance. Continuing in this way could create a powerful trance force which would implement the suggestion even at a distance. If there were no trance force created, then there would be no effect.

Designing a trance that works means that you must be careful as to what the content of the trance generating loop is in terms of secondary effects.

The content of the trance generating loop is absolutely not a factor in creating a primary dissociation and a meditation trance, but the content of the trance generating loop can be an important factor in converting the meditation to a addiction hypnotic trance and will act as a suggestion to modify the dissociated trance plane. For example, with the dissociated trance plane subsequently modified second order trance generating loops may be created, or the primary dissociated trance plane could become disabled and the trance would stop.

Using the principles of trance engineering, here is an example which might have meaning for you. If you are working in a place that is not pleasing to you, you might have, at some time in the past, said to yourself "I hate this place; I hate this place; I hate this place." This repetition, repeated in your mind, will induce a trance. However, in the trance that is created, you are doing yourself a disservice by practicing bad trance engineering. What you produce with this trance generating loop is anger, frustration and disappointment. The trance force, if any is created, would repel most people, even people that could help you. Instead, use some of the principles of good trance engineering. Say to yourself, "What a joke; what a big joke; what a big fucking joke." The effect of this emotionally triggered trance generating loop will, among many other effects, bring a smile to your face as well as others. This effect, like magic, could change some of the characteristics of that place that you seemed to hate.

Back to magic

The first order trance generating loop may not be easily accessed even if known.   One may become aware of the existence of strong trance forces by being aware of a certain 'weirdness'. That is, the presence of a strong trance force will tend to pull new people also into the same trance. Those who are generating such forces may seem to have a type of charisma or 'magnetic personality'. This is indicative of the potentiating effect of the trance force.

It is important to understand that the mechanics of trance really has nothing to do with the personality or ethics of the operator, magician, yogi, dentist, shaman, priest, psychiatrist, politician, hypnotist, witch, salesman or saint, *per se*.

So far, we have been discussing trance which has been created through loops which occur solely in the mind.   I would now like to extend this idea to structures or mental schema which are more abstract but which are also linked to the mind through trance forces.

If the schematic associative paths in the mind were known and could be explicitly described, then the corresponding state of consciousness would be known. These associative schema are really nothing more than the electrochemical paths, thus, an interesting possibility arises that if a trance force is applied to associated schema, then it should be possible that the corresponding state of consciousness will be potentiated.

To change any structure requires the expenditure of energy. If a structure could be explicitly described as above, by enumerating the paths, then the energy needed to change any potential structure could be derived.

One of the most important forms of changing psychic structure is "learning". Learning, whether it be new information, created material, or being convinced of an idea, likewise requires the expenditure of energy by a source. This force is related to the energy required in the target to change the psychic structure plus the loss associated in transferring the structure across space.

The more obscure or subtle the information to be learned, the more energy is necessary to change or to create the psychic structure in the target sufficient to hold the associated network representing the new information.

Potentiating thinking in a new mode then could occur simply by traversing the "ego" along the nodes of the new structure. This observation has an application in the use of trance forces.

Any cybernetic structure is an inductive trance force. That is, a cybernetic structure, like a trance force, will potentiate a force within reality and cause a structure to duplicate itself. This is what is meant by inductive and in this sense, the trance force induces change in reality. A trance force sets up compelling or potentiating forces by the nature of its structure. That is, consciousness potentiated by a trance force must traverse the path along all similar nodes of the path. Variance from the path of the trance force requires that consciousness expend energy to "break" the trance force. However, if consciousness succeeds in traversing along a path not specified by the structure of the trance force, the trance force "vanishes". I can hypothesize then, that it must be the structure of the trance force itself which generates the constraining forces to consciousness. If the constraining forces were absent, then consciousness would change. That is, consciousness would then reflect the change in the underlying structure.

A trance force structure will duplicate itself under induction. Primarily, the trance force structure must be cybernetic. Second, the trance force structure must be transformable to some type of pattern in evolution and must function in an area where the cybernetic trance force structure is free to operate. I would be then that the structure would potentiate and replicate itself.

Powerful yogic trance states are often created by the long term practice of meditation. Short term meditation trances are qualitatively different from long term meditation trances. The reason for this is that the ability to maintain higher intensity trance forces becomes easier and more conscious with time. This may account in part for the differences in the spectacular effects that are reputed to yogis and the impossibility of scientists to replicate them.

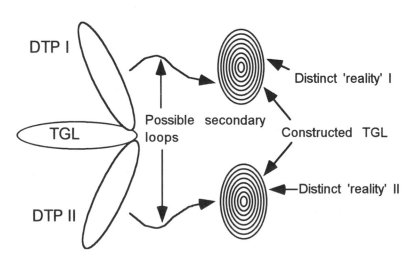

Figure 5: Showing how separate realities can result from multiple dissociated trances.

Trance results from a repetition or looping of consciousness. When the content of the trance has achieved a resonance, which is to say that the intensity of the trance can be maintained most efficiently, special types of psychic forces are generated which are called trance forces. The effects of these special psychic forces are often falsely identified with the behavior which produced them and even more so with the person with whom they are most closely identified.

When you realize how trances are produced and what the effects of trances can be, it may be sufficient to simply note that a particular person was employing efficient trance techniques in order to generate strong trance forces.

Trance — for a yogi or a magician — is merely a tool consciously chosen and made efficient over years of consistent practice to produce specific psychic results. Trance — for most other people — is an unconscious choice made to relieve pain or to avoid uncomfortable feelings or situations.

The critical difference in these trances is that yogic trances are created deliberately with the trance generating loop entirely in the mind of the yogi. Most other people slip into trances because they become the elements of other peoples trance generating loops and therefore become subject — like pawns — to manipulations.

Contacting other worlds, the unseen worlds of plants and animals, for example, requires a special type of awareness. Some cognitive functions must be disabled and others must be enabled.

The magic circles of magicians and witches are structures of trance forces and only one gross effect is that they limit the attention of the witch; more subtly, such potentiated circles are inductive and both create dissociated trances planes at a distance from the circle and construct other patterns. The patterns which are constructed are exact copies of the potentiated dissociated trance plane patterns established by the witch. Depending on other local and global trance forces, these constructed patterns will dissipate. Since most trance forces that are created in this way are weak, the constructed patterns usually quickly dissipate. In the cases where local and global trance forces are supportive of the potentiated trance force, the patterns are quickly established.

That is to say, it is easy to do magic to create rain in a rain storm. It is possible to influence the weather by magic alone if the trance force is strong enough.

The strength of the trance force depends on being able to create and to skillfully manipulate simultaneously two or more dissociated trance planes, to sustain them for long periods of time, to change their forms, and to modulate them. This must be done without the practitioners destroying his ego structure and creating psychotic delusions or addictions.

A model, such as this one, only has value so far as it is useful and practical.

Knowing how to recognize trances, how to analyze trance and to work with its components is only the first step in using trance in magical and shamanistic ways. There are many dangers that follow from the use of trance to create alternate dissociated trance planes with the intent that these dissociated trance planes potentiate generating trance loops.

Delusions and the Breakdown of the Ego Structure

I have been describing fundamental and somewhat normal or usual trance types. Because trance generating loops are practically not constant, their dissociated trance planes are also not constant. In normal cases, this is not a problem. However, when trance generating loops consist of highly charged triggers and when secondary loops also contain triggers, multiple dissociated trance planes may be created.

A normal ego structure may occasionally go into a trance or dissociate for a short period of time. However, when multiple dissociated trance planes exist with stabilizing secondary loops, the combined realities of the dissociated trance planes may exceed the reality of the normal ego structure. In such a case, the individual's realities are the hallucinations and memories taking place in the dissociated trance planes, with one or more planes appearing to be real. Such a structure would represent a very real breakdown of the normal ego structure with the concomitant delusions clinically found in psychotics.

When the dissociated trance planes are carefully constructed over a period of time, and with a good understanding of trance engineering, it becomes possible to create more shamanistic, healing or magical trances rather than schizophrenic or psychotic trances.

One of the main differences between a schizophrenic and a shaman is that the shaman at least maintains some normal ego structure so that it is possible for the shaman to consciously manipulate the dissociated trance plane forces in service of healing. This is what people call shamanic 'magic.' The schizophrenic has lost this ego structure and has very little control over the dissociated trance planes. In such a condition, the schizophrenic is delusional and may be frightened of the hallucination and may react in relation to the hallucinations rather than any normal appearances of reality.

Terminating a Trance

Because trances may be created without knowledge or intent, it is critical to understand the detailed mechanics of trance and to discover specifically what trances are enabled in an individual. Some trances may be terminated or replaced with other trances either with or without the permission or knowledge of the subject.

In order to terminate a trance, you must first know what type of trance it is you wish to terminate. Simple trances are easy to terminate. More difficult are the trances that are of long duration or which have secondary loops. Life long trances and addictive or centric trances with multiple secondary loops are extremely difficult to terminate.

Terminating a meditative trance is fairly easy. Only the trance generating loop needs to be interrupted. If there is no secondary order trance generating loop, then interrupting the primary trance generating loop will terminate the trance. If there is a secondary order trance generating loop then that secondary order trance generating loop must be interrupted first. Interrupting the primary trance generating loop will not be effective because the secondary order trance generating loop will reestablish it immediately.

Terminating a hypnotic trance can also be easy. You can interrupt the secondary trance generating loop or you can also disturb the primary trance generating loop by intervention. Talk over the television, for example, or simply turn it off.

Terminating an addictive trance is more difficult because there is not too much access to the primary trance generating loop, since it is in the dissociated plane. Practically, there are multiple secondary trance generating loops. It is possible to manipulate or substitute the external stimulation and to perturb the trance generating loops to such an extent that the dissociated trance planes will break down. Sometimes you can drug switch, which is precisely substituting one external component for another. However, merely substituting one drug for one other drug is not enough to break the secondary order trance generating loop or the dissociated trance planes which are derived from them especially if the substituted drug also creates trance effects. In order to really terminate the trance, the external components must be substituted so often that there is real instability in the dissociated trance planes or that so many other dissociated trance planes are created that the trance forces become weaker and dissipate. By monitoring the dissociated trance planes and discovering their weak points, a therapist or analyst can learn how individual trance addictions can be terminated. It can be argued that merely substitution of one drug for another is not an ethical approach to trance termination. It can also be an abuse. From this perspective, groups such as Alcoholics Anonymous which substitute a religious addiction for an alcohol addiction are not really solving the addiction, but are merely drug switching. It could be argued that this is an abuse of the potential of the addicted individual and is merely a more socially acceptable form of codependency.

Social responsibility concerns raise the hope that pathological and addictive trances would always be replaced with more benign trances or at least the individual would be empowered to manipulate his own trances. Empowering the individual to control their own trances is one purpose of this book.

Trance therapies would ideally work to terminate trance, or if terminating a trance is simply too scary, then to replace pathological trances with more benign trances.

The ostensible goal of spiritual consciousness raising activities is to terminate trances, but often only trance replacement occurs. In the worst cases benign trances become pathological or delusional but with the label 'spiritual.' Several examples of this are the religious terrorists and the suicidal "martyrs for God."

Trances which result from secondary order trance generating loops are extremely difficult to break. Deep hypnotic trances will always be found to have secondary order trance generating loops. One strategy for breaking such trances is to attack the second order trance generating loops first. It is my opinion that attacking the first order trance generating loops will be very difficult without first modifying or destroying the second order trance generating loop.

Start at any place in your trance. Addictive trances reward an impoverished thought-set. You can help reduce the effects of any trance by rewarding the enrichment of your thoughts. This means to expand the variety of your thoughts without trying to remove the thoughts you think are the problem. Continue expanding and enriching your thoughts with new and stimulating ideas, people and experiences. When the variety of your thoughts becomes robust, ideas will be self-generating and the trance will naturally cease to exist by definition.

Many trances are like 'bad habits', but really bad ones; an idea or behavior which is repeated without awareness. Replacing one habit with another does not break the trance, it is simply replacing one trance generating loop with another. The dissociated trance plane may or may not be the same! What is more effective is to increase the number of elements in the trance generating loop, or to add complexity to the trance generating loop. The idea is to make the trance generating loop unstable so that the dissociated trance plane cannot be sustained.

There is an opportunity to develop many new strategies for breaking these trances using the trance model. A trance analysis is the primary requirement to identify the first and second order trance generating loops.

Like many technologies once well understood, trance can be used for good or for evil and by anyone willing to employ the techniques and willing to invest the time and energy in order to develop conscious control over the trance forces.

So long as trance is generally poorly understood then it is possible that shamsters can exploit this ignorance by making false claims that the content of the trance generating loops actually has something to do with the effects being produced.

The Future of Trance Technology

The development of trance technology will certainly demand that many human activities be examined as to their trance characteristics. Once specific human activities have been analyzed for trance, it becomes possible to modify behavior in conscious ways.

Every new technology carries with it additional responsibility. This is also true for trance technology. Any technology can be quite dangerous for the immature. Trances are dangerous enough for people who get caught in a trance without knowing what is happening to them. Those who consciously manipulate people into trances for which there may be no escape or which have secondary effects have committed a serious injury and should be held culpable at law. What comes to mind in this regard is the television trances which feed the hypnotized subjects endless images of violence. Such hypnotized subjects are without doubt potentiated to commit future violence and the producers of such images should be held culpable for any such violent acts as though they had committed it themselves.

Good applications of trance technology would include new diagnostic and therapeutic strategies. Analysis of current therapeutic strategies from a trance technology point of view would likely result in more effective strategies. It may be that a simple trance analysis would expose counterproductive strategies when trance or behavior modification is a desired outcome. I could imagine that the careful construction of trances could bring the hope of new possibilities or skills in people who had particular disabilities.

With the careful development of the use of trance force, some naturally skilled witches, magicians or shamans might be particularly effective resources in bringing about results in situations that would normally be very difficult or impossible to resolve.

Conclusion

There is enough information in this small book to start people thinking in a new direction about trance. No doubt, some of the ideas here might later be proven to be wrong or imprecise; but this is the possibility of any highly speculative theory. However, if my specific personal and empirical researches are correct, then I suspect that generally the structure of the trance model should be valid. There are many specific examples which suggest this is so. If the model and the ideas are substantially correct, then there are many important implications to be taken which would affect the way we deal with trance.

I have only lightly touched on many diverse aspects of trance. In a preliminary book like this, I felt that it was more important to make broad outlines of the subject rather than delve into too many details or show all the possible applications. The trance model as expressed here provides opportunities for future research. I welcome serious comments on the issues I may have raised.

Human behavior can be changed and controlled by means of trance. This is nothing new; it is already happening worldwide with television, religion and so on. What may be new is that trance technology will help make this control more effective because trance theory is a more of a precision instrument in a field where there is a lot of controversy about trance. I do not advocate that there should be more control; this is just the inevitable reality of the introduction of any new technology.

What might be hoped for is that trance theory will be used for trance analysis and trance termination rather than trance enhancement. Trance enhancement is like a power drug and when abused impoverishes human potential; but there are many people who are fascinated by trance, power, and drugs and who will abuse power. In this sense and use, trance theory would be dangerous.

The future of trance technology, therefore, has great potential for good as well as for evil. Trance, but not trance theory, is already being used by many people and groups and established commercial and social institutions in both ways, so this is nothing new. What is new is that by becoming aware of how trance works in this more precise form, as described here, you may have both the analytical tools for recognizing the poison as well as the possibility of finding the antidote. You should also become aware of the real and imaginary prisons that are possible with trance. It is this knowledge, perfected by long, careful and efficient practice, which can either potentiate you or destroy your worlds whether you are a priest, a therapist, a magician, a politician or a psychotic.

A Final Warning

Creating multiple dissociated trance planes is potentially very dangerous. Addictive, centric and other types of trances can have serious and permanently damaging effects on the ego structure. Therefore, I would seriously and emphatically warn those who would experiment with these advanced trance forms, to be extremely cautious.

Bibliography

Agrippa von Nettesheim, Heinrich Cornelius. *Three Books of Occult Philosophy.* (Tyson, Donald, ed) St. Paul: Llewellyn Publications, 1993.

Aitchison, Jean. *The Articulate Mammal: An Introduction to Psycholinguistics.* New York: Universe Books, 1976.

Asher, "Respectable hypnosis," *British Medical Journal,* 1:309-312, 1956.

Baker, Robert A., *They Call It Hypnosis,* New York: Prometheus Books, 1990.

Bandler, R., & Grinder, J. *The Structure of Magic I.* Science and Behavior Books, Palo Alto, 1975.

Bandler, R., & Grinder, J. *The Structure of Magic II.* Science and Behavior Books, Palo Alto, 1976.

Barber, T. X., "Physiological effects of 'hypnosis,'" *Psychological Bulletin,* 58:390-419, 1961.

Barber, T. X., "Physiological effects of 'hypnotic suggestions': a critical review of recent research (1960-1964)," *Psychological Bulletin,* 63:201-222, 1965.

Bartis, S. P., & Zamansky, H. S. "Dissociation in hypnotic amnesia," *American Journal of Clinical Hypnosis,* 29:103-108, 1986.

Bowers, K. S. "Unconscious influences and hypnosis" in J. L. Singer (ed) *Repression and Dissociation* (143-178) Chicago: University of Chicago Press, 1990.

Clawson and Swade, "The hypnotic control of blood flow and pain: The cure of warts and the potential for the use of hypnosis in the treatment of cancer," *American Journal of Clinical Hypnosis,* 17:160-169, 1975.

Coleman, Daniel, *The Varieties of the Meditative Experience,* 1977.

Dukhan, H., & Rao, K. R. "Meditation and ESP scoring." *Research in parapsychology 1972.* Metuchen, NJ: Scarecrow Press, 1973.

Edwards, "Duration of post-hypnotic effect," *British Journal of Psychiatry,* 109:259-266, 1963.

Edwards, Betty. *Drawing on the Right Side of the Brain: A Course in Enhancing Creativity and Artistic Confidence.* Tarcher/St. Martins Press, 1979.

Erickson, M. H., Rossi, E. L, & Rossi, S. I., *Hypnotic Realities: The Induction of Clinical Hypnosis and Forms of Indirect Suggestion*. New York: Irvington Publishers, 1976.

Erickson, M. H., Rossi, E. L., *Hypnotherapy: An exploratory Casebook*. New York: Irvington Publishers, 1979.

Fromm, Erika and Nash, Michael R. (ed.), *Contemporary Hypnosis Research*. New York: The Guilford Press, 1992.

Gilligan, Stephen G., *Therapeutic Trances: The Cooperation Principle in Ericksonian Hypnotherapy*. New York: Brunner/Mazel, 1987.

Gorassini and Spanos, "A sociocognitive skills approach to the succesful modification of hypnotic susceptibility," *Journal of Personality and Social Psychology*, *50*:1004-1012, 1986.

Grey Walter, M. *Megabrain*. New York: Ballantine, 1991.

Grinder, John and Bandler, Richard (ed. Connirae Andreas), *Trance-Formations: Neurolinguistic Programming and the Structure of Hypnosis*, Utah: Real People Press, 1981.

Haley, J. (Ed.) *Advanced Techniques of Hypnosis and Therapy: Selected Papers of Milton H. Erickson*. New York: Grune and Stratton, 1967.

Hamilton, Max. *Psychosomatics*. New York: John Wiley & Sons, 1955.

Hammond, D. Corydon (Ed). *Handbook of Hypnotic Suggestions and Metaphors*. New York: W. W. Norton, 1990.

Heeb, Donald O., *The Organization of Behavior*, 1949.

Heller, Steven & Steele, Terry Lee, *Monsters and Magical Sticks: there's no such thing as hypnosis?* Scottsdale: New Falcon, 1991.

Hilgard, E., "Dissociation and theories of hypnosis" in *Contemporary Hypnosis Research*. New York: The Guilford Press, 1992.

Hilgard, E. R., *Divided consciousness: Multiple controls in human thought and action*. New York: Wiley, 1977.

Hodgson, R. "A record of observations of certain phenomena of trance." *Proceedings of the Society for Psychical Research*, *8*:1-167, 1892.

Horner, A. & Buhler, C. "Existential and humanistic psychology: A hope for the future in philosophy," *Psychotherapy and Research*. International Psychiatry Clinics, *6*(3):55-73, 1969.

Ittelson, W. H. & Kilpatrick, F. P. *Experiments in Perception the Nature of Human Consciousness: A Book of Readings*. Ornstein, R. (Ed.) San Francisco: W. H. Freeman, 1973.

Janet, P. *Psychological Healing: A Historical and Clinical Study*. New York: Macmillan, 1925.

Kawano, Kimiko, "Fractal dimensional analysis of EEG during hypnosis," in *Contemporary International Hypnosis* Chichester: John Wiley & Sons, 1995.

Klatzky and Erdely, "The response criterion problem in tests of hypnosis and memory," *International Journal of Clinical and Experimental Hypnosis, 33*:246-257, 1985.

Klippstein, Hildegard (Ed). *Ericksonian Hypnotherapeutic Group Inductions.* New York: Brunner/Mazel 1991.

Kroger, Wm. S. & Felzler, Wm. D. *Hypnosis and Behavior Modification: Imagery Conditioning.* Philadelphia: Lippincott, 1976.

Kroger, Wm. S. *Clinical and Experimental Hypnosis.* Philadelphia: Lippincott, 1963.

Kuhn, S. S., *The Structure of Scientific Revolutions.* Chicago: University of Chicago Press, 1962.

Laubscher, B. *Sex customs and psychopathology: A study of South African pagan natives.* New York: McBride, 1938.

Loftus and Loftus, "On the permanence of stored information in the human brain," *American Psychologist, 35*(5):409-420, 1980.

Luria, A. R. *The Working Brain.* New York: Basic Books, 1973.

Lynn, Steven. & Rhue, Judith. (ed) *Theories of Hypnosis: Current Models and Perspectives.* New York: Guilford Press, 1991.

Mander, Jerry. *Four Arguments for the Elimination of Television.* New York: William Morrow/Quill, 1977.

Maslow, A. H. *The Farther Reaches of Human Nature.* New York: Viking Press, 1971.

McClelland, J. K., & Rumelhart, D. E. *Parallel Distributed Processing: Explorations in the Microstructure of Cognition.* Cambridge: MIT Press, 1986.

McKenna, Terence and Dennis. *The Invisible Landscape: Mind Hallucinogens and the I Ching.* San Francisco: Harper San Francisco, 1993.

Miller, G. A., Galanter, E., and Pribrim. K. H. *Plans and the Structure of Behavior.* New York: Holt, Reinhart and Winston, 1960.

Oestrander, S., Schroeder, L., and Oestrander, N. *Superlearning.* London: Book Club Associates, 1984.

Orne, M. T. "The nature of hypnosis: Artifact and essence." *Journal of Abnormal and Social Psychology. 58,* 277-299, 1959.

Ornstein, R. E. *The Psychology of Consciousness.* San Francisco: W. H. Freeman, 1972.

Penfield, W. & Roberts, L. *Speech and Brain Mechanisms.* Princeton: Princeton University Press, 1959.

Rulison, "Warts, A statistical study of nine hundred and twenty one cases," *Archives of Dermatology and Syphilology, 46*:66-81, 1942.

Shevrin, H. & Dickman, S. "The Psychological Unconscious: A necessary assumption for all Psychological Theory?" *American Psychologist, 35*(5):421-434, 1980.

Spiegel, D. "Dissociating damage." *American Journal of Clinical Hypnosis, 29*:123-131, 1986.

Stava, K. J., & Jaffa, M. "Some operationalizations of the neodissociation concept and their relationship to hypnotic susceptibility." *Journal of Personality and Social Psychology, 54*:989-996, 1988.

Tart, Charles (ed.), *Altered States of Consciousness*. New York: Doubleday/ Anchor, 1972.

Tart, Charles T., *States of Consciousness*. New York: Dutton, 1975.

Ullmari & Dudek, "On the psyche and warts: II. Hypnotic suggestion and warts," *Psychosomatic Medicine, 22*:68-76, 1960.

Ullman, M., "Herpes Simplex and second degree burn induced under hypnosis," *American Journal of Psychiatry, 103*:828-830, 1947.

Van Gorp, Meyer, and Dunbar, "The efficacy of direct versus indirect hypnotic induction techniques on reduction of experimental pain," *International Journal of Clinical and Experimental Hypnosis, 33*:319-328, 1985.

Wagstaff, G. F., *Hypnosis, Compliance, and Belief*, New York: St. Martin's Press, 1981.

Weitzenhoffer, A. M. *General Techniques of Hypnotism*. New York: Grune & Stratton, 1957.

Wells, W., "The extent and duration of post-hypnotic amnesia," *Journal of Psychology, 9*:137-151, 1940.

Wier, Dennis R., "A suggested basis for literary evaluation by computer processing," *Journal of Aesthetics and Art Criticism, 26*:47-52, 1967.

Wilson and Barber, "The fantasy prone personality: Implications for understanding imagery, hypnosis, and parapsychological phenomena," *Imagery, Current Theory, Research, and Application*, New York: Wiley Press.

Wolberg, L. R. *Hypnoanalysis*. New York: Grune and Stratton, 1964.

Wolinsky, Stephen. *Quantum Consciousness*. Connecticut: Bramble Books, 1993.

Wolinsky, Stephen. *The Tao of Chaos: Essence and the Enneagram*. Connecticut: Bramble Books, 1994.

Wolman, B. *Dictionary of Behavioral Science*. New York: Van Nostrand Reinhold Co, 1973.

Yapko, Michael D., *Hypnotic and Strategic Interventions: Principles and Practice*. New York: Irvington Publishers, 1986.

Young, J. Z., *Programs of the Brain*. Oxford: Oxford University Press, 1978.

Index